D0064812

A PATH TO
REDEEMING LOVE

A PATH TO

Redeeming Love

A 40-DAY

DEVOTIONAL

FRANCINE RIVERS

WITH KARIN STOCK BUURSMA

MULTNOMAH

Published in the United States by Multnomah, an imprint of Random House, a division of Penguin Random House LLC. Portions of this text originally appeared in *Redeeming Love,* copyright © 1997 by Francine Rivers, published in the United States by Multnomah, an imprint of Random House, a division of Penguin Random House LLC, in 1997. The 1997 edition is the "redeemed" version of *Redeeming Love,* published by Bantam Books in 1991; the original edition is no longer available.

MULTNOMAH® and its mountain colophon are registered trademarks of Penguin Random House LLC.

Library of Congress Cataloging-in-Publication Data
Names: Rivers, Francine, 1947– author.
Title: A path to Redeeming love : a forty-day devotional / Francine Rivers.
Description: First edition. | [Colorado Springs] : Multnomah, 2020.
Identifiers: LCCN 2020008821 (print) | LCCN 2020008822 (ebook) |
ISBN 9780525654346 (hardcover) | ISBN 9780525654353 (ebook)
Subjects: LCSH: Rivers, Francine, 1947– Redeeming love. | God (Christianity)—Love. |
Devotional literature, American.
Classification: LCC PS3568.I83165 R583 2020 (print) | LCC PS3568.I83165 (ebook) |
DDC 242/.2—dc23
LC record available at https://lccn.loc.gov/2020008821

Printed in the United States of America on acid-free paper

waterbrookmultnomah.com

2 4 6 8 9 7 5 3 1

First Edition

SPECIAL SALES
Most Multnomah books are available at special quantity discounts when purchased in bulk by corporations, organizations, and special-interest groups. Custom imprinting or excerpting can also be done to fit special needs. For information, please email specialmarketscms@penguinrandomhouse.com.

CONTENTS

INTRODUCTION

Hosea's story in the Bible had a great deal to do with my decision to give my life to Jesus Christ. I had grown up in the church, but like others, I was able to sit in the pews for years and never allow my heart to be touched by the gospel. Knowledge is fine, but it's love that transforms us, Christ's love. After I studied the book of Hosea, I saw how patient and how deep God's love is for me—and everyone. How could I not fall in love with God through His Son, Jesus? Why had I rebelled and resisted for so long?

At this point in my life, I'd been writing love stories for almost ten years and realized how much deeper God's love is for us than what we read in romance novels or see in romantic movies. God's love is a consuming fire! His passion for each of us is beyond our understanding. His love is so high, deep, and wide that it necessitated the blood sacrifice of His own Son to atone for our sins to make the way open to Him. The love He offers each of us is forever strong. It never wavers with feelings or circumstances. He is faithful, trustworthy, and the lover of our souls, offering us a marriage consummated by the indwelling of the Holy Spirit. When we say yes to Jesus, we are *in* Christ, sealed and secure no matter what happens. He will never lose us.

While studying the book of Hosea, I felt the Lord nudging me to write His love story. The prophet's life gave me the plot. As I studied God's character in order to develop the character of Michael, I prayed readers would see the difference between what I had been writing about (*eros,* or sensual love) and what real love looks like—passionate, sacrificial, unchanging, and eternal. When readers wrote to me and said they longed to meet a man like Michael, I would write back, "You can! His name is Jesus!" This is why I wrote *Redeeming Love:* so that you would know how greatly you are loved and that no matter what you've been through, God loves and wants you. He can make beauty out of ashes. He makes all things new.

Karin Buursma and I have worked together to take the truths of God's never-ending love that are highlighted in the novel and expand them into a devotional format. Each devotion begins with a scene from *Redeeming Love,* tracing Angel's journey from despair and rejection to rescue, redemption, and ultimately full restoration. We pull out key spiritual themes in the story—such as the gift of hope, the reality of God's presence with us even in hard times, and the transforming power of God's forgiveness—and consider what they mean in our own lives.

The devotions are grounded in Scripture because we want to continually point you back to God's Word. It is our best source of truth about what God is really like and how He wants to interact with His people.

While our circumstances are undoubtedly different than Angel's, we all share the essence of her journey. We too often feel rejected, believing no one can love us for who we are. Our past hurts, along with a distorted understanding of God, can hold us back from fully embracing His love and believing that He can redeem the hard things in our lives. Our prayer is that when you finish reading this book, you'll be able to see more clearly who God is and how He is calling you to be restored in Him. May the truth of God's redeeming love bring you hope and joy as you draw closer to Him.

REJECTED

W E ALL EXPERIENCE REJECTION. Sometimes it strikes in subtle ways, and other times in a blatant way. I look back over my life and remember the pain of it. When I was a small child, I stood in the doorway of my mother's room as she told me, from her bed, to stay out of the room and away from her. I retreated, crushed and convinced that my mother didn't love me. Other mothers hugged and kissed their children. Mine didn't. The only person I saw my mother kiss was my father. That early rejection was the first and most severe, but others followed:

- I felt like an outcast because all the popular students lived in town and I lived a couple miles away.
- I was bullied and called names.
- I heard people refer to the rural road on which I lived as "chicken alley."

- Girls sneered at my homemade dresses and hand-me-downs from cousins.
- I strove to win an end-of-summer swim contest, only to have the blue ribbon go to my visiting cousin.
- I had a giant crush on a boy who liked girls who were prettier and smarter than me.
- I didn't have the necessary test score or grades to make it into the college that was my first choice.

When I was a little girl, I cried over being rejected. By fourth grade, I learned to pretend it didn't hurt. I became better at swallowing rejection as I grew up. Don't most of us try to walk through the pain until it dissipates?

Rejection is a wound. Sometimes it heals quickly. Sometimes it takes years. In either case, it doesn't take much to re-open the wound, to feel afresh the lacerating pain and trickling blood. Sometimes rejection becomes an infection that sickens and weakens a life.

Yet sometimes there is another side to the rejection we experience, a side we would never guess until light shines on it and we seek the love and acceptance we have longed for since the womb.

DAY 1

Longing for Approval

ALEX STAFFORD STARED down at Sarah. His mouth was pressed tight, and he studied her silently. Sarah stood as still as she could. She'd stared at herself in the mirror so long this morning, she knew what he would see. She had her father's chin and nose, and her mother's blonde hair and fair skin. Her eyes were like her mother's, too, although they were even more blue. Sarah wanted Papa to think she was pretty, and she gazed up at him hopefully. But the look in his eyes was not a nice one. . . .

The parlor window was open, and she could hear voices. Sarah wanted to sit and listen to her parents. That way she would know just when Papa wanted her to come back again. If she was very quiet, she wouldn't disturb them, and all Mama would have to do was lean out and call her name.

"What was I to do, Alex?" her mother said. "You've never spent so much as a minute with her. What was I to tell her? That

her father doesn't care? That he wishes she had never even been born?"

Sarah's lips parted. Deny it, Papa! Deny it!

We long for approval from those we admire. But what happens when we don't get it?

Sarah had idolized the idea of her father for years. She hoped he would love her the way she had always dreamed he would. That he would be proud of her, would pay attention to her, would even delight in her. The truth she overheard— that her father wished she had never been born—crushed her. And Alex's rejection had far-reaching shadows. His words seeped into Sarah's heart and formed the deepest truths she believed about herself: she was worthless and unloved, and it would have been better if she had never existed.

Rejection is a heavy burden for any person—child or adult—to bear. Yet we all carry it. Whether this burden came from a parent or a friend, a teacher or a peer, we have all experienced moments when others have weighed us in the balance and let us know, by their demeaning words, scornful looks, or excluding actions, that they have found us insufficient.

What words of rejection have sunk deep into your heart?

- "I don't love you anymore."
- "You're not pretty enough or smart enough."
- "You're boring."
- "No one likes you."

When we don't care about the speaker, these words can roll off our backs. We shrug or roll our eyes, and the cruel words are gone. Forgotten. But more often these words linger in our minds and become part of us. We pull them back out and examine them again and again, and each time we do, we believe them a little more.

Over time, our brains can turn "I don't love you" into "No one will ever love you." "You're not good at this" can become "You're just not good enough" and then "You're worthless." The messages become broader, encompassing more of us and eroding our sense of worth. We wonder if our lives are mistakes.

How do we move forward if we let others' rejection of us define us? A psalm of David speaks truth over these lies:

> You formed my inward parts;
> You wove me in my mother's womb.
> I will give thanks to You, for I am fearfully and
>   wonderfully made;
> Wonderful are Your works,
> And my soul knows it very well.
> My frame was not hidden from You,
> When I was made in secret,
> And skillfully wrought in the depths of the earth;
> Your eyes have seen my unformed substance;
> And in Your book were all written
> The days that were ordained for me,
> When as yet there was not one of them.
>   (Psalm 139:13–16)

These words speak powerfully of how God created us, fashioning us deliberately. Do you wonder if it's a mistake that you're alive? *God formed your inmost being and has ordained your days.* Do you question your own worth? *You are fearfully and wonderfully made.* Do you feel you are hopelessly flawed? *God wove you together.* Do you feel unknown and alone? *God sees you.*

Sarah's father considered her a mistake, an annoyance, a burden he wished to be rid of. Her mother loved her imperfectly, viewing her as an obstacle to Alex's affection. But the way her parents saw her didn't line up with who she really was.

The deepest truth about us is that we are created by God. We are loved. We are known and seen. Even beyond that, God delights in us!

The way Zephaniah 3:17 portrays God is almost startling:

The LORD your God is living among you.
    He is a mighty savior.
He will take delight in you with gladness.
    With his love, he will calm all your fears.
    He will rejoice over you with joyful songs. (NLT)

If the One who created us delights and rejoices in us, we can know that we're never unwanted or worthless, no matter what anyone else says. If you're struggling with feeling rejected, let others' harsh words turn you toward the only One whose acceptance matters. Let the truth of *His* words sink deep into your heart and permeate all aspects of who you are. You are valuable. You are wanted. You are loved.

Meditate on Psalm 139:13–16, and consider what the verses tell you about how you were deliberately created. What messages of rejection in your mind can this replace?

DAY 2

A World Devoid of Kindness

CLEO TOOK A long drink and swallowed down the tears and misery and let the bitterness and anger rise and flow. "All men want to do is use you. When you give them your heart, they tear it to shreds. None of 'em care."

Sarah stared at her with wide frightened eyes. She trembled violently. Cleo eased her grip. "Your mama told me to take good care of you," she said. "Well, I am going to take care of you. I'm going to tell you God's truth. You listen and you learn." She let go and Sarah sat very still.

Glaring at the little girl, Cleo dropped into the chair by the window and took another swig of rum. She pointed, trying to steady her hand. "Your fine papa doesn't care about anyone, least of all you. Sooner or later, he's going to get tired of your mama and toss her into the trash. And you with her. That's the one thing you can count on."

Sarah was crying now, and she reached up to wipe tears from her cheeks.

"Nobody cares about anybody in this world," Cleo said, feeling sadder and more morose by the second. "We all just use each other in one way or another. To feel good. To feel bad. To feel nothing at all. The lucky ones are real good at it. Like Merrick. Like your rich papa. The rest of us just take what we can get."

⌘

When we see the world through the lens of our experiences, our view can end up horribly distorted.

Eight-year-old Sarah's comfortable world had already started to crumble around her when she met her father and realized he was not the man she'd hoped he'd be. It crumbled further when her mother sent her away with Cleo, who clearly found her a burden and wished she wasn't there. Already feeling rejected and alone, Sarah was hit hard by Cleo's bitter speech. It made her question all she knew about life, including the warmth and love she had experienced with her mother. Was none of it real? Did no one in this world genuinely care for anyone else?

In our bleakest moments, many of us have asked these questions too. When we feel desperately alone, we wonder if genuine compassion even exists. We become cynical, assuming others have selfish motives for everything they do. Thinking this way has ramifications for our hearts. When we believe the world is a cold place that runs on selfishness and rejection, we begin to turn inward. We trust no one. How can we? No one cares, everyone is looking out for herself, and kindness is an illusion.

We come to believe a significant lie: we have to watch out for ourselves because nobody else will look out for us.

We find a beautiful antidote to this lie in Scripture:

Zion said, "The LORD has forsaken me,
And the Lord has forgotten me."
"Can a woman forget her nursing child
And have no compassion on the son of her womb?
Even these may forget, but I will not forget you.
"Behold, I have inscribed you on the palms of My
      hands." (Isaiah 49:14–16)

The Lord doesn't gloss over the fact that human relationships fail. Some of us have experienced rejection or indifference from those who should love us most, and it hurts us deeply. But even then, even in the worst circumstances, we are not abandoned to make our own way in the world. God Himself will *never* forget us. Our names are permanently marked on His hands. He loves us "with an everlasting love" (Jeremiah 31:3). God's care and compassion for us have no end.

Yes, we will encounter people who hurt us, forget us, or try to use us for selfish ends. Those realities are part of the fallen world we live in, and we grieve because of it. But that's not all there is. The world cannot operate wholly on selfishness because it was created and is ruled by a God who operates on love. In those times when we feel rejected, when we wonder whether anyone cares, and when we struggle to see glimpses of love and goodness in the people around us, we must turn to God and let Him recalibrate our worldviews.

Cleo thought she was telling God's truth, but her view was distorted by her own painful circumstances. Isaiah 40:11 presents a compelling picture of what the world is *really* like for those who trust in God:

> Like a shepherd He will tend His flock,
> In His arm He will gather the lambs
> And carry them in His bosom;
> He will gently lead the nursing ewes.

If you wonder whether there is any love or altruism in the world, hold on to this image of God caring for you as tenderly as a shepherd leads his sheep and carries them close to his heart.

When we feel alone, rejected by people's unkindness or indifference, we can remember that God's love, not people's selfishness, is ultimately the driving force in our lives. When we believe this, we can let go of the need to protect ourselves and to always look out for our own interests. When we're convinced that God has our backs, we are freed from fear of rejection and can live at peace in the reality of His unchanging love.

Reread Isaiah 40:11 and visualize the scene. Meditate on the reality that God cares for you as tenderly as a shepherd cares for his sheep.

DAY 3

Seeking Forgiveness

WHEN THEY REACHED *the door, Mama took a deep breath and knocked. A woman came to answer. She was small and gray and wore a flowered gingham dress covered by a white apron. She stared and stared at Mama and her blue eyes filled with tears. "Oh," she said. "Oh.* Oh . . . "

"I've come home, Mother," *Mama said.* "Please. Let me come home."

"It's not that easy. You know it's not that easy."

"I've nowhere else to go. Please, Mama."

The lady opened the door and let them in. She showed them into a small room with lots of books. "Wait here and I'll speak with your father," *she said and went away. Mama paced, wringing her hands. She paused once and closed her eyes, her lips moving. The lady came back, her face white and lined, her cheeks wet.* "No," *she said. One word. That was all.* No.

Have you ever desperately needed mercy and received none? That kind of rejection causes a deep wound that is slow to heal.

Sarah's mother was desperate. Years ago, she had gone against her parents' wishes and everything she'd been taught, leaving it all behind for a man who wasn't her husband. Love—or what she thought was love—blinded her to everything else. She ignored the warnings and ran headlong down a path that turned out to be a dead end. The handsome, charming man she chose lacked basic decency and kindness. Eventually, he abandoned her. She returned home to throw herself on her parents' mercy, asking if she could move back in.

They said no.

It didn't matter to them that she was sorry. It didn't matter that she acknowledged they had been right all along. It didn't matter that Sarah, an innocent child, would suffer. And it didn't matter that in refusing shelter to their daughter, they were condemning her to an even worse fate, making it inevitable that she would become the very thing they most feared. She had made a mistake, and now she had to pay. There was no going back. No forgiveness. No mercy. Only rejection that hurt Sarah to her core.

We've all felt the weight of unforgiveness. At the very moment we need mercy most—when we're hyperaware of our own failings and the heaviness of our wrong choices is almost more than we can bear—we look for someone who can help us move forward. Someone who will extend grace and love us despite what we've done. Someone who will tell us that all is not lost. That there's a way out of what seems like a dead end and that our wrong choices will not define us forever.

But too often that's not what happens. People can't resist reminding us of what we've done, rubbing our sin in our faces. We hear the messages loud and clear:

- "I told you so."
- "You made your bed; now you have to lie in it."
- " 'Sorry' isn't good enough."
- "It's too late."

Our imaginations may not be big enough to see there is more to the story. But God isn't done yet, and our imperfect choices don't have to be the end.

Psalm 103 paints a beautiful picture of God's mercy:

The LORD is compassionate and gracious,
Slow to anger and abounding in lovingkindness.
He will not always strive with us,
Nor will He keep His anger forever.
He has not dealt with us according to our sins,
Nor rewarded us according to our iniquities.
For as high as the heavens are above the earth,
So great is His lovingkindness toward those who fear Him.
As far as the east is from the west,
So far has He removed our transgressions from us.
    (verses 8–12)

"He has not dealt with us according to our sins." God, in His mercy, does not keep reminding us what we've done wrong after we've confessed it. He does not sit back, uninvolved, and watch us suffer the consequences of our sins. He responds to us with compassion, giving us more than we deserve—more love, more grace, more mercy.

He has not "rewarded us according to our iniquities." God does not operate on a barter system, making us pay for what we did through penance or suffering. He responds to our repentance with grace and compassion, abounding in love.

"As far as the east is from the west, so far has He removed our transgressions from us." This doesn't mean we don't deal with consequences, but it does mean that after we have come to Him in repentance, God doesn't continue to hold our sin against us. He forgives us and lets the past go.

"The LORD is compassionate." His response is not to shame or reject us. Instead, He loves us.

If you're stuck in unforgiveness and rejection, realize those traps are not from God. People might fail to extend mercy, but God will not. Their harshness can remind us to find our forgiveness in Him, for He promises us forgiveness. He promises that when we come to Him, overwhelmed with our own sin and grief, He will lighten our load and extend mercy to us.

Reread Psalm 103:8–12. Picture God picking up your sins and bad choices and taking them far away—so far that you will never see them again.

DAY 4

What Good Is God?

THE MEN BEGAN *wrapping Mama in a sheet.*

"Wait a minute," said one, and pried the rosary from Mama's fingers and dropped it in Sarah's lap. "I bet she woulda wanted you to have that, honey." He finished the stitching while Sarah ran the beads through her cold fingers and stared at nothing.

They all went away, Mama with them. Sarah sat alone for a long time wondering if Rab would keep his promise to take care of her. When night came and he didn't come back, Sarah went down to the docks and flung the rosary into a garbage scow. "What good are you?" she cried out to the heavens.

No answer came.

She remembered Mama's going to the big church and talking to the man in black. He talked a long time, and Mama had listened, her head bowed, tears running down her cheeks. Mama never went back, but sometimes she would still sift the beads through her slender fingers while the rain spat on the window.

"What good are you?!" Sarah screamed again. "Tell me!"

❦

What good are You, God? If we're honest, who among us has not asked this question to some degree? We might have asked it apologetically, with less anger than Sarah, but we all ponder what difference God's presence actually makes in our lives.

Sarah asked this question after seeing her mother's life fall apart and end in despair—despite all her prayers for help. Now Sarah was alone, a helpless child with only a drunk to watch over her. She felt abandoned and rejected. Again. What good was God? Had He turned His back on her?

We might doubt God's care because of a crisis in our own lives: the death of someone we love, a financial setback, or a painful rift in an important relationship. So many things seem to go wrong, leaving us frustrated, exhausted, and confused. If we are trusting God, why doesn't He fix our problems and save us from these crushing struggles? Why should we follow Him if we don't receive any tangible benefits? Where is He? Has He rejected us?

Scripture doesn't provide easy answers for the *why* questions we all face. But the Bible does give us truths to cling to while we ask them.

Psalm 34:18 gives this promise: "The LORD is near to the brokenhearted and saves those who are crushed in spirit." And Deuteronomy 31:8 tells us, "The LORD is the one who goes ahead of you; He will be with you. He will not fail you or forsake you. Do not fear or be dismayed."

When we are at our lowest—overwhelmed, broken-hearted, crushed in spirit—He is nearest. He knows how we feel. He cares. He is with us, supporting us and walking alongside us in our trials.

His presence doesn't answer all our questions. It doesn't take away our problems or make everything okay. Life can still be soul-crushingly hard. But one of God's greatest gifts is that we do not have to go through it alone. No matter how difficult, no matter what the circumstances, and no matter whether our problems are of our own making or not, the God of the universe is with us.

Struggles will be an integral part of life as long as we're alive, so don't let yourself believe that your challenges mean that God has rejected you. Instead, focus on the fact that He is the God who cares deeply in the midst of the challenges. Second Corinthians 1:3–4 says, "Blessed be the God and Father of our Lord Jesus Christ, the Father of mercies and God of all comfort, who comforts us in all our affliction." We may not fully understand what God is doing, but we can trust His heart of love and comfort.

John 11 tells the story of Jesus arriving in the town of Bethany after His friend Lazarus had died. When our Lord saw Lazarus's sister Mary and others with her grieving, He joined them.

> When Jesus therefore saw her weeping, and the Jews
> who came with her also weeping, He was deeply moved
> in spirit and was troubled, and said, "Where have you

laid him?" They said to Him, "Lord, come and see." Jesus wept. So the Jews were saying, "See how He loved him!" (verses 33–36)

What's extraordinary is that even though Jesus knew He was going to raise Lazarus from the dead in mere minutes, He didn't rush to the miracle. He took time to grieve over Lazarus's death and acknowledge the sorrow of his friends and family. The pain was meaningful, even when the final result was going to be reversed.

When you wonder where God is or whether He cares, picture Jesus—full of compassion—weeping at Lazarus's tomb. He grieves with those who grieve. He stays near, and He comforts us in all our troubles.

Memorize Psalm 34:18 or Deuteronomy 31:8. When you feel overwhelmed or discouraged today, repeat the verse to yourself and remember that God is with you in the midst of trouble.

RESIGNED

R ESIGNATION MEANS GIVING IN to something unpleasant that one can't change. We encounter resigned people every day. We see the hopelessness in their eyes and hear it in their voices. They are like walking wounded, putting one foot in front of the other, playing out their time on this planet. Resignation says, "This is the way life is. We grow up, work hard, grow old, and die."

After having an abortion during my college years, I resigned myself to living with regret for having committed what I believed to be an unforgivable sin—taking my child's life. It didn't matter how many people told me, before or after the abortion, that I'd made "the right decision" or that "it" wasn't really a child yet anyway. I knew the truth. My choice left me with an emptiness I couldn't fill.

I thought about suicide. My death would be just and right,

wouldn't it? I'd taken a life. Therefore, my life should be forfeited. But fear held me back. I believed my choice would consign me to hell, and I didn't want to go there. I thought it better to stay alive and bury the memory, guilt, and shame deep enough that I might be able to forget. After all, there could be no going back and changing what I'd done. What other choice was there but to live with the pain?

The truth was like a stone dropped in the bottom of my heart, sending ripples of consequences through my life. Rick felt it, too, even though he had no part in my decision. When Rick and I lost three of our children to miscarriages, he grieved but I felt resigned. I deserved to lose my children, didn't I?

Resignation can smother hope, breed depression, and strip away joy. Resignation can become surrender to captivity. It sets a course for the long haul through life. It's embracing this idea: "This is the way things are. Nothing is going to get better. It's my fault."

It's not always our choices that lead to resignation. At times it can happen because of what is done *to* us, and it masks itself as a matter of survival.

A girl or boy is kidnapped or seduced, then raped, trafficked, and held in bondage.

A soldier is severely wounded during war.

A fire sweeps away homes and possessions, changing the landscape of an entire town.

Earthquakes, floods, wars, market crashes, illnesses, or deaths of loved ones—so many things are outside our control. But do we have to *bear* life? Wouldn't we rather *live* it?

With all the things that can and often do happen, how we endure is still a decision. No matter the circumstances, life doesn't have to be ruled by resignation. And, impossible as it may seem, surrender can be the very decision that brings cleansing fire, new life, and the joy we long to experience.

DAY 5

Hoping in God

HOSEA DID COME back, the next night and the next. Each time Angel saw him, her unrest grew. He talked, and she felt desperation stirring. She knew better than to believe anyone about anything. Hadn't she learned the hard way? Hope was a dream, and reaching for it turned her life into an unbearable nightmare. She wasn't going to get sucked in by words and promises again. She wasn't going to let a man convince her there was anything better than what she had.

Yet, she could not dispel the tension that rose each time she opened her door and found that man standing outside it. He never laid a hand on her. He just painted word pictures of freedom that resurrected the old, aching hunger she had felt as a child. It was a hunger that had never died. Yet each time she had run away to find an answer to it, disaster had fallen upon her. And still, she had kept trying. The last time, the hunger had sent her running from Duke and landed her here in this foul, stinking place.

Well, she had finally learned her lesson. Nothing ever got better. Things only went from bad to worse. It was wiser to adjust and accept and survive.

⚜

What happens when we lose hope?

Angel's hope had been chipped away, bit by bit, by years of trauma. Rab. Duke. Johnny. The women who attacked her on the ship. The men who appeared night after night. One disappointment after the next. One person after another who let her down and didn't have her best interests at heart. Men who tried to win her trust and then just used her for their own pleasure. Her heart was hard. She was resigned to life as she knew it, and her hope had been almost extinguished.

But not quite. No matter how hard she tried to ignore the pang and push it far down inside, she still hungered for something different—something better. She longed for freedom from everything that bound her, and she hoped that one day life could be different, that the world could be a friendlier place than she had known so far.

Proverbs 13:12 tells us, "Hope deferred makes the heart sick, but desire fulfilled is a tree of life." When we wait and wait for something we hope for, we become jaded. We can't even imagine that anything will change. Stuck and hopeless, we become resigned to life as it is now—an existence that's as good as it's ever going to get. We're taught painful lessons by life, and we decide it's better to expect nothing. At least that way we won't be disappointed.

But the spark of hope within us will not be extinguished.

Hope is a gift that God gives us even in the direst circumstances, a whisper inside us that says, "This is not all there is." And the Holy Spirit keeps that spark of hope alive.

Psalm 146:3–6 reads,

> Don't put your confidence in powerful people;
>   there is no help for you there.
> When they breathe their last, they return to the earth,
>   and all their plans die with them.
> But joyful are those who have the God of Israel as their
>   helper,
>   whose hope is in the LORD their God.
> He made heaven and earth,
>   the sea, and everything in them.
>   He keeps every promise forever. (NLT)

If what we place our hope in is weak, the outcome won't be good, no matter how much faith we have. But if the object of our hope is strong, the outcome is certain, even if our faith is weak. The psalmist exhorts us to put our hope in the only One who will not fail: God, who remains faithful forever.

When we hope in people, as Angel did, we will be disappointed. When we put our hope in ourselves—our own competence, talents, reputations, or charisma—we will be disappointed. We're not powerful enough or skilled enough to control our destinies and deliver on all our promises. But when we put our hope in God, as the psalmist tells us to do, we find certainty.

Romans 5:4–5 talks about "our confident hope of salvation" and tells us that "this hope will not lead to disappointment. For we know how dearly God loves us, because he has given us the Holy Spirit to fill our hearts with his love" (NLT). Our hope in God is sure because He keeps all His promises, He is all-powerful, and He loves us more than we can imagine.

When you are certain that life can't get better—that you're stuck forever with your regrets, your hard circumstances, your suffering—remember that even if your faith is weak, God, the object of your faith and hope, is sure.

What area of your life makes you feel most hopeless? Take a moment to talk to God about it. How can you hold on to the hope that will not disappoint?

Fear of the Unknown

WHAT WAS KEEPING her here? Why didn't she just walk out the door?

Her hands balled into fists. She would have to get her gold from the Duchess first, and she knew there was no way the woman would give over all of it at once.

And what if Angel did have enough gold to leave? It could turn out the same way it had on the ship or at the end of the voyage when she had been beaten and left behind for those scavengers to find. Those few days on her own in San Francisco had been the closest thing to perdition she had lived. She had been cold, hungry, afraid for her life. She had looked back on life with Duke with actual longing. Duke, of all people.

Desperation filled her. I can't leave. Without someone like Duchess, or even Magowan, they would tear me to pieces.

She didn't want to risk going with Michael Hosea. He was by far a darker unknown.

❧

Resignation builds on fear, and fear keeps us trapped.

By any measure, Angel's life was terrible. She was essentially kept as a prisoner by the Duchess, forced to work as a prostitute yet never given the money she'd earned. The threat of mistreatment was always present—if not from the paying guests, then from Magowan, who constantly lurked on the periphery. Angel's dream of independence was a fantasy; unless something changed, her only future was continuing in prostitution as long as men found her attractive and, after that, working as a servant in the brothel or living on the streets.

Michael Hosea offered marriage and a home. Angel had already observed his kindness and integrity. She had every reason to go with him and absolutely no reason to stay—yet she could not bring herself to leave behind what was familiar and embrace the unknown. Fear immobilized her.

Fear is a constant companion for some of us. It looks over our shoulders as we make decisions and invades our thoughts as we consider the future. When we lie down at night, it overwhelms our minds with worries about all the things that could go wrong. We fear making mistakes, losing the good opinion of others, or suffering the illness or death of those we love. And while we sometimes fear the things we know, our biggest fears are reserved for the unknown. We imagine a myriad of different outcomes for our situation, most of them terrible. We let our minds run amok and then find ourselves paralyzed, unable to act or make good choices because we're afraid of what might happen.

A surprising number of verses in the Bible address fear, and many of them command us, "Fear not!" Psalm 46:1–3, 7 says:

> God is our refuge and strength,
>> always ready to help in times of trouble.
> So we will not fear when earthquakes come
>> and the mountains crumble into the sea.
> Let the oceans roar and foam.
>> Let the mountains tremble as the waters surge! . . .
> The Lord of Heaven's Armies is here among us;
>> the God of Israel is our fortress. (NLT)

This passage is notable for what it *doesn't* say: that God will make everything work out okay for us. There's no such promise. Instead, the psalm paints a picture of drastic circumstances. The earth could be shaken by such a great earthquake that the very mountains would break off and fall into the raging ocean—yet the psalmist says he will not fear. How is that possible?

Verses 1 and 7 answer this question: because God is with us.

This isn't just any god we're talking about. This is the Lord Almighty, the God of Jacob. He is the creator of the universe and the one who has redeemed us through Christ's death on the cross. He is the one who is our refuge, our strength, and our fortress. He is the one who has promised not to leave us.

We fear the unknown, but what is hidden from us is known by God. Isaiah 46:9–10 reads,

Remember the things I have done in the past.
>   For I alone am God!
>   I am God, and there is none like me.
Only I can tell you the future
>   before it even happens.
Everything I plan will come to pass,
>   for I do whatever I wish. (NLT)

Nothing is a mystery for God. He already knows what will happen in the future, and He already knows how He will help us through it.

If you're resigned to stay where you are because you're too afraid to move forward, you don't have to give in to that fear. Fight back by reminding yourself with each breath that God is with you and nothing is too hard for Him. Slow down your anxious thoughts by remembering that He knows the outcome already. And hold on to the truth that He knows what is best for you.

When we're stuck, His presence can give us courage to move forward.

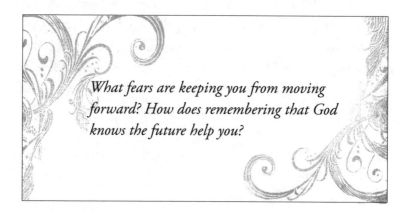

What fears are keeping you from moving forward? How does remembering that God knows the future help you?

No Way Out

ANGEL'S MIND FLASHED back to a tall dark man in a black evening suit. It came to her with sudden finality that there was no way out, not for her. There never had been; there never would be. Everywhere she turned, every time she tried, she was trapped again, worse off than before.

Hopeless rage filled her. She remembered everything ever done to her from the time she was a child in a shack on the docks to now, in this room. It was never going to get any better. This was all she could ever expect of life. The world was full of Dukes and Duchesses and Magowans and men to come line up outside her door. There was always going to be someone to enslave and use her, someone to profit from her flesh and her blood.

There was one way out.

Resignation, taken to the extreme, brings us to despair. The morsel of hope that Michael Hosea had held out to Angel was beginning to seem real. Sick of her life, she wondered if she really could start over. She pulled out the dream of a little house in the country, a place where she could live on her own, finally in peace. Fueled by her dream and growing unrest with the way things were, she approached the Duchess to ask for her gold. But when the conversation turned hostile and the Duchess sent Magowan after her, the weight of resignation pulled Angel down. Nothing would ever change, and there was no use trying. The only option left was to give up hope altogether—and let Magowan kill her so she would finally be out of her misery.

Despair comes when our last hope is gone and we don't see a way out of our circumstances. Sometimes it comes when we're overwhelmed by regret over a bad decision. Sometimes it comes as a result of abuse we experienced, a wrong done to us, or just the sheer number of smaller things that weigh us down every day until we feel as if there's no escape. If you've ever struggled with depression, suicidal thoughts, or unrelieved anxiety, you know what it's like to feel that the last glimmer of light is receding and leaving you alone in the darkness. Maybe you've been fighting against it for a long time, but now you have no more energy left to resist. It feels as if all you can do is give in.

Scripture doesn't shy away from talking about despair or any of the bleakest emotions, for that matter. Job, after losing his family and his possessions, cursed the day of his birth and wished it would disappear from the calendar forever. David wrote psalms in his darkest moments, including these words from Psalm 69:

Save me, O God,
For the waters have threatened my life.
I have sunk in deep mire, and there is no foothold;
I have come into deep waters, and a flood overflows me.
I am weary with my crying; my throat is parched;
My eyes fail while I wait for my God. (verses 1–3)

And Jesus, while on the cross, uttered this heartrending expression of despair: "My God, my God, why have you forsaken me?" (Matthew 27:46, NIV).

When we're at the point of our greatest despair, isn't our greatest fear that God has abandoned us? Because if He has left us alone, all hope is lost. Nothing will ever change.

But our God is present in the dark places.

The accuser may tell us that we are alone, abandoned, and in hopeless darkness. But that is a lie. In our utter despair, we may feel that there is no way out. But that is a lie too. *God is with us.* And because He is there, we are never entirely in the darkness. Whether we can see it or not, there is always a pinprick of light.

The apostle John described Jesus this way: "The Word gave life to everything that was created, and his life brought light to everyone. The light shines in the darkness, and the darkness can never extinguish it" (John 1:4–5, NLT).

The darkness tries to overcome the light—and tries hard. We've all experienced this, both in our own lives and in the pain and chaos we see in the world. But we have the guarantee of God Himself that darkness will not succeed. No matter what, His light will endure—because He Himself is the light and nothing can overcome Him.

John 8:12 records these words of Jesus: "I am the Light of the world; he who follows Me will not walk in the darkness, but will have the Light of life." When you feel the darkness closing in, cling to these verses and remember the truth. No matter how difficult things are, how bad things seem, or how hopeless you feel, the truth is that all is not lost. God is present. And where He is, there is hope. His light will not be extinguished.

Picture a candle with a flickering flame. No matter what happens—air blowing, water splashing, a snuffer taking away all the oxygen—the candle keeps burning. How does this image of inextinguishable light give you hope?

The Possibility of Change

"MY NAME ISN'T Mara. It's Angel. You ought to get the name right if you're going to put the ring on my finger."

"You said I could call you anything I wanted."

Men had called her by other names than Angel. Some nice. Some not so nice. But she didn't want this man calling her anything but Angel. That's who he had married. Angel. And Angel was all he was going to get.

"The name Mara comes from the Bible," he said. "It's in the Book of Ruth."

"And being a Bible-reading man, you figure Angel is too good a name for me."

"Good's got nothing to do with it. Angel isn't your real name."

"Angel is who I am."

His face hardened. "Angel was a prostitute in Pair-a-Dice, and she doesn't exist anymore."

"Nothing's any different now from what it's always been, whatever you choose to call me."

"Things will be different now." Has anyone ever said that to you, or have you ever said it to yourself? Every now and then we succeed in finding a new path, but more often than not, real change doesn't happen. Good intentions give way to old habits. New patterns slip away before they ever had a chance to be established. In the end, nothing really changes.

Angel was sure nothing would ever be different for her either. She had tried to start a new life—by running away from Duke, by coming to California, by trying to strike out on her own, by trusting another person—but in the end, all her striving had come to nothing. She still ended up stuck in a life she hated. Now Michael had pulled her out of that life, but she was sure it was too late. Maybe she wasn't living in Pair-a-Dice anymore, but she couldn't escape the well-worn patterns she'd established. She didn't trust anybody, and she assumed all those around her were only out for whatever they could get for themselves. How could she find a new way to live?

On our own, it's almost impossible to make lasting changes that affect the core of who we are. Oh, we might be able to adjust our habits if we have enough willpower and motivation. We can start eating healthy foods or working out regularly. We can get up earlier, journal more often, and complete more items on our to-do lists. But down deep, we're still the same people—just more organized, fitter, or healthier versions of them. Only God can change us at the deepest level.

The apostle Paul knew this truth firsthand. His life was sharply divided into two phases: before and after he met Christ.

Before that day on the road to Damascus (Acts 9), Paul's main driving force was his zeal for God's law. Proud of his education and background as a Pharisee, he watched approvingly while Stephen, one of Jesus's followers, was killed for blasphemy. Saul, as Paul was known then, "was going everywhere to destroy the church. He went from house to house, dragging out both men and women to throw them into prison" (8:3, NLT).

But one moment with Jesus changed the trajectory of Saul's life. Saul soon possessed a new understanding of who God was, a new name, and a new purpose. His life became completely centered on Jesus. Through years of travel and hardship, his one goal remained: sharing the gospel with the Gentiles.

Paul experienced change from the inside out. God transformed him from being driven by pride and anger to being driven by love, from being intent on destroying others to being focused on preaching the life-giving gospel at every turn. His zeal remained, but God transformed it for His glory.

We all have patterns of thought and behavior that we think we're trapped in because they're just too deeply ingrained. But God has the power to make us new creatures in Him.

Paul wrote to the church at Corinth about people who deliberately sin in different ways, but then he added, "Such were some of you; but you were washed, but you were sanctified, but you were justified in the name of the Lord Jesus Christ and in the Spirit of our God" (1 Corinthians 6:11). The Corinthians had been dramatically changed, from thieves and slanderers and drunkards to redeemed followers of Christ. We have been changed too—in the name of Jesus and by the Spirit of God—and we will continue to be changed until the day Jesus returns and we see Him in heaven. Our transformation is part of the "now and not yet." When we trust in Christ, we are justified by faith and made right before Him, but we're still in the process of being fully sanctified. Change is happening now *and* later.

If you feel stuck today, caught in a rut that you'll never be able to escape, then picture Paul. Remember that he was a former murderer and persecutor who threw men and women in prison just for believing in Jesus. And then remember that he became the most dedicated missionary the world has ever seen, one who was beaten and jailed and eventually executed for sharing the gospel. If God can change someone like Paul, He can change people like us. We don't have to be resigned to life as it is when our powerful God is working in us to show us life as it can be.

What patterns in your life do you think will never change? How does thinking about Paul help you more fully understand God's power to transform?

Learning to Surrender

"*YOU CAN'T EXPECT to get it perfect the first time. It takes practice.*" Like cooking stew, he wanted to say. Like living a different way of life.

Kneeling closer, Angel laid the fire just as he had done. She did it exactly right, then struck the flint and steel. She made a spark, but it didn't catch. She tried again, more resolute, and failed. Her burned hand hurt abominably, but she clutched the tools with such absolute determination that her palms began to sweat. With each failure, her chest ached more, until the pain was so permeating, so deep and disabling, that she sank back on her heels.

"I can't." What was the use?

Michael's heart ached for her. "You try too hard. You expect to do everything right. It's not possible."

What happens when we're not good enough?

Faced with a new way of life on the farm, Angel had to develop a different set of skills. But learning new things was harder and slower than she expected. When she didn't get things right away—heating the stew, building a fire—she gave up. Dejected, she took her failure as one more piece of evidence that she was unable to change. She would never adapt to farm life. She would never be an adequate wife. She would never be good enough.

So many of us get stuck wanting to be good enough. We try our hardest to win approval through what we do. We think if we can just live perfectly, others will like us, no one will be upset with us, and we'll finally feel better about ourselves. Even God might like us better if we finally stop messing up. But no matter how hard we work, we can't do everything right. And then, face to face with our failure, we wonder why we even bothered. Resigned, we feel worthless and think we should just give up altogether.

The good news of the gospel is that God already knows we can't do it right. Our mistakes and failures never surprise Him. He releases us from the burden of trying to be perfect, because He Himself is perfect.

Paul wrote this to the Ephesians:

> God is so rich in mercy, and he loved us so much, that even though we were dead because of our sins, he gave us life when he raised Christ from the dead. (It is only by God's grace that you have been saved!) For he raised us from the dead along with Christ and seated us with him in the heavenly realms because we are united with

Christ Jesus. So God can point to us in all future ages as examples of the incredible wealth of his grace and kindness toward us, as shown in all he has done for us who are united with Christ Jesus.

God saved you by his grace when you believed. And you can't take credit for this; it is a gift from God. Salvation is not a reward for the good things we have done, so none of us can boast about it. (2:4–9, NLT)

This beautiful vision of the gospel calls us not to be resigned but to *surrender*.

When we're resigned, we accept something that's unpleasant, believing we're trapped where we are and life will never improve. We lose hope.

Surrendering, on the other hand, means letting go of ourselves—of our pride and our attempts to be good enough on our own—and grabbing hold of God. When we surrender, we stop trusting in our own righteousness and instead trust in His. Instead of *resigning* ourselves to something painful or negative, we *surrender* to God, which is the best possible thing we can do because He will lead us to what is best for us.

To surrender to the gospel, we need to acknowledge that we're incapable of being fully righteous on our own and earning our salvation. Accepting *that* truth is not the gateway to despair. Instead, it's the gateway to hope. We're accepting that we need God and believing He has already provided for that need.

God loved us "even though we were dead because of our sins." He made a way for us even when we were failing, imperfect, and full of ugliness and sin. He has seen it all, yet He calls us to Himself.

In Matthew 11, Jesus offered a beautiful invitation:

Come to Me, all who are weary and heavy-laden, and I
will give you rest. Take My yoke upon you and learn
from Me, for I am gentle and humble in heart, and you
will find rest for your souls. For My yoke is easy and My
burden is light. (verses 28–30)

Jesus's yoke is light because He is not expecting us to be
perfect. He doesn't command us to follow His law without a
single misstep, to make everyone happy, or to gain all the ac-
colades. Instead, He calls us to follow Him, trust Him, and
depend on His grace for our salvation. He calls us to let go of
our desire for perfection in ourselves and instead celebrate His
perfect righteousness, which is enough for us.

If you're feeling weary and burdened, struggling to let go
of your own efforts, then surrender to God, asking Him to
help you remember your need for Him. The yoke of perfection is heavy, and we'll never be able to carry it. But the yoke
of surrender is light.

*What do you think is the difference between
surrendering to God and being resigned? In your
life, what do you need to surrender to God?*

The Life God Offers

BEFORE HER WAS *light: pale yellow growing brilliant, gold-streaked with red and orange. She had watched sunrises before from within walls and behind glass, but never like this, with the cool breeze in her face and wilderness in every direction. She had never seen anything so beautiful. She felt Hosea's strong hands on her shoulders.*

"Mara, that's the life I want to give you. I want to fill your life with color and warmth. I want to fill it with light."

Her mouth curved into a sad smile, and her soul ached. Maybe this man was all he seemed. Maybe he meant every word he said, but she knew something he didn't. It was never going to be the way he wanted it. It just couldn't happen. He was a dreamer. He wanted the impossible from her. Dawn would come for him, too, and he would awaken.

Angel didn't want to be anywhere around when he did.

❦

W hat kind of life do we think God wants to give us?

In the early hours of the morning, Michael took Angel on a long walk to the top of a hill, where they waited. She wondered why—until the dawn broke and a glorious sunrise spread across the sky. It was far more beautiful than anything she'd ever seen and more magnificent than she could have imagined.

"That's the life I want to give you."

How often do we think of the life God offers as one of beauty? In our distorted understanding, we might be more likely to think He offers a life of duty or guilt. Maybe we think following God will be hard work and spoil our fun, or we think that we'll lose everything we love. We drag our feet when it comes to following Him because we're focused on what we're giving up. But how often do we think about what He's really offering us?

Jesus's words in John 10:10 hint at what He promises us: "The thief comes only to steal and kill and destroy; I came that they may have life, and have it abundantly." *Abundant life.* God does not skimp on grace. He does not give us the bare minimum of what we need. He gives us infinitely more than enough, more than we can even imagine.

In 1 Corinthians, we read,

No eye has seen, no ear has heard,
     and no mind has imagined
what God has prepared
     for those who love him. (2:9, NLT)

It's hard for us to believe God has such wonderful plans for us. Raised in this world, surrounded by failure and pain—in our own lives and the lives of those around us—we are always waiting for the next disaster to hit. Like Angel, we might smile sadly at other people's optimism when they talk about God's good gifts and what God has planned, but we're not so sure. We might think, *Everything good we've ever enjoyed has had an ending, so why should we expect anything different in the future?*

Because God's promises are certain.

In this fallen world we will have sorrow and pain, but we will also experience grace and forgiveness and love and joy. We have the promise that God will never leave us, no matter what happens. And we have the promise that one day, when all things are made right, we will taste what God has prepared for us—which will be far more glorious than anything we could ever imagine.

Revelation 21:3–4 gives us a glimpse of this future, and even just this glimpse is amazing:

> I heard a loud voice from the throne, saying, "Behold, the tabernacle of God is among men, and He will dwell among them, and they shall be His people, and God Himself will be among them, and He will wipe away every tear from their eyes; and there will no longer be any death; there will no longer be any mourning, or crying, or pain; the first things have passed away."

Our future involves life in God's presence, life that's without sorrow or death but is full of joy. We will see God and know Him. We will be a part of His eternal kingdom. We will know life as it is supposed to be.

When you're struggling through doubt or despair, look for someone who can point you to this truth and remind you that what you see now is not all there is. Ask God to give you a glimpse of the life of faith and joy He wants you to enjoy.

We don't need to keep bracing ourselves for the bad things to come. We can rest in the truth that God is moving all things toward this glorious future. We may be in darkness now, but the sunrise is coming. And it will be beautiful.

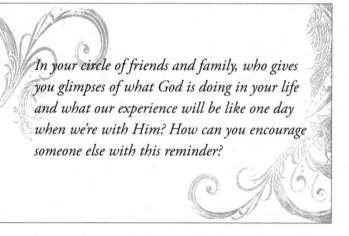

In your circle of friends and family, who gives you glimpses of what God is doing in your life and what our experience will be like one day when we're with Him? How can you encourage someone else with this reminder?

Undone by Love

ALL THE WAY *back, she had imagined Michael gloating and taunting, rubbing her face in her own broken pride. Instead, he knelt before her and washed her dirty, blistered feet. Throat burning, she looked down at his dark head and struggled with the feelings rising in her. She waited for them to die away, but they wouldn't. They stayed and grew and made her hurt even more.*

His hands were so gentle. He took such care. When her feet were clean, he kneaded her aching calves. He cast the dirty water outside and poured more, setting the pan in her lap. He took her hands and washed them as well. He kissed her stained, scratched palms and worked salve in. Then he wrapped them with warm bandages.

And I hit him. I drew his blood . . .

Angel shrank back ashamed. "Why do you do this for me?" she said thickly. "Why?"

⟋⟍⟋⟍⟋⟍

A genuine act of love can change everything.

Afraid of her growing feelings for Michael, Angel decided to leave while she still could. She started back to Pair-a-Dice to get the gold she was owed, but she ended up lost and cold. When she finally returned home, chilled, dirty, and exhausted, Michael's response shocked her. Instead of reacting with anger and violence, he responded with love and compassion that she knew she didn't deserve. He fed her, warmed her, and cleaned her up. His tender care touched her deeply.

Selfless love is powerful. Selfless love—godly love—gives without expecting anything back and gives to those who don't love in return. That runs contrary to our very human nature.

Left to ourselves, many of us are more likely to live as if we're maintaining a detailed spreadsheet. We keep track of the pluses and minuses as closely as if our lives were part of a complicated personal accounting system. *I did him a favor, so now he owes me.* From little concerns like who did the dishes or drove the carpool to big issues like who inflicted the last betrayal and what the retribution will be, the record keeping is exhausting. Whether we're cataloging our faults or others', we become slaves to them, unable to let any actions pass without calculating their effects on the bottom line. We want to get what we're owed, and we don't want to be beholden to anyone because that gives others power over us.

Love gets rid of all that. God's record keeping is different.

Romans 6:23 tells us "the wages of sin is death, but the free gift of God is eternal life in Christ Jesus our Lord." In the biggest way of all, God doesn't give us what we deserve. He withholds the consequences we should receive because of our sin and gives us a mind-blowing gift instead. Not death, but eternal life. Not condemnation, but grace. Not separation from Him, but His loving presence.

How do we respond to that kind of grace?

If we're stuck in a legalistic mindset, we might find this grace frightening. We can control our mental spreadsheet and keep track of what we owe, but grace is something else entirely. If we, like Angel, are resigned to the idea that we can't change, we might be terrified by the idea that we could owe something to God that we can never repay. What kind of power might that give Him over us? How might He use it against us?

The apostle Peter refused one of his first tastes of grace. In John 13, at the beginning of the Last Supper, we read that Jesus began to wash all the disciples' feet—a task usually reserved for servants. The Bible doesn't record the way the other disciples responded, but Peter's reaction was firm. We read,

> When Jesus came to Simon Peter, Peter said to him, "Lord, are you going to wash my feet?"
>
> Jesus replied, "You don't understand now what I am doing, but someday you will."
>
> "No," Peter protested, "you will never ever wash my feet!" (verses 6–8, NLT)

Imagine your pastor or boss coming to wash your feet or do another menial task for you. Being served by one we can't repay feels uncomfortable, and many of us would rather avoid it altogether. But Jesus didn't let Peter do that.

Jesus replied, "Unless I wash you, you won't belong to me."

Simon Peter exclaimed, "Then wash my hands and head as well, Lord, not just my feet!" (verses 8–9, NLT)

Why was it important for Peter to let Jesus wash his feet? Because accepting grace is a fundamental part of the gospel. We can't earn our salvation; we must admit our helplessness and let God save us, knowing that we'll be forever in His debt.

But God is not a frightening creditor. Just as Michael gave to Angel without expecting anything back, God gives to us freely. He knows we can't repay, and He will not hold our debt against us. Romans 11:35–36 says, "And who has given him so much that he needs to pay it back? For everything comes from him and exists by his power and is intended for his glory. All glory to him forever! Amen" (NLT).

If you find yourself stuck in the spreadsheet mentality, keeping track of what you owe and who owes you, you can find freedom in letting it go and embracing grace.

Is the idea of grace frightening to you? How could giving up your record keeping help you respond with love instead of resignation?

DAY 12

Voices of Condemnation

PAUL CAUGHT HER arm tightly, and she looked at him again, her face pale. He glared into her cynical blue eyes. "Well, you do. You owe me for this ride." He let her go abruptly.

Angel felt the spiraling begin inside her. Going down, like water in a sinkhole. She had forgotten that everything cost something. She let her breath out and tilted her head slightly. "Well, we might as well get it done."

Furious, he grabbed her arm and propelled her a hundred feet off the road, into the shadows of a thicket. He was rough and quick, his sole desire to hurt and degrade her. She didn't make a sound. Not one.

"Didn't take you long to fall back into old ways, did it?" He glared down at her in disgust.

Regret, if not prompted by God, leads to condemnation. When Paul returned to the farm, his presence upset the balance Angel had found with Michael. Just as she was beginning to get a glimpse of herself as Michael saw her, Paul showed up and his reaction snapped her back to reality.

Angel understood Paul. From him she received exactly the treatment she expected: condemnation, anger, and disgust. All her sins and faults were laid bare before his eyes, and he told her precisely what he thought of her. It hurt, but it didn't surprise her. He treated her exactly the way she thought she deserved. Once again, she was reminded that life would never change. She believed no one could ever see her as anything other than a prostitute because that's what she was on the inside. Enmeshed in that hopelessness, Angel couldn't imagine that saying no to Paul's demand for payment was even an option. Everything cost something, so she paid her debt.

Resignation can steep us in regret and drag us down the well-worn path of condemnation. Have you been there? The words we say to ourselves can be horrifying in their directness. *You're awful. You'll never do anything right. No one really cares about you. You're worthless.* These ugly words do not reflect God's truth.

When we're stuck in self-condemnation, our best antidote is truth from Scripture. Romans 8 begins with this promise: "There is now no condemnation for those who are in Christ Jesus. For the law of the Spirit of life in Christ Jesus has set you free from the law of sin and of death" (verses 1–2).

When we trust in Christ, we are set free from the law of sin and death by the Spirit who gives life. We're no longer judged according to what we've done but by whom we trust. Praise God!

No condemnation from the only One who is qualified to condemn. None.

Others may criticize us and try to condemn us, but they don't have the right. Those who condemn the loudest might be the same ones who are trying the hardest to cover up their own sin. Paul was the one who forced Angel's return to prostitution, yet he absolved himself and blamed her. Uncomfortable with his own actions, he closed his eyes to his own sins—his treatment of her, his betrayal of Michael—and decided it was all her fault.

That's not God's way. In a familiar passage from the gospel of John, a woman caught in adultery was brought before Jesus and accused. Jesus told the Pharisees, "He who is without sin among you, let him be the first to throw a stone at her" (8:7). After they all left, one by one, Jesus asked, " 'Woman, where are they? Did no one condemn you?' She said, 'No one, Lord.' And Jesus said, 'I do not condemn you, either. Go. From now on sin no more' " (verses 10–11).

The Bible is clear that all humans have sinned, so none of these accusers had grounds to throw a stone. But here's the bigger point: Jesus could have condemned the woman. He was free from sin, so by His own criteria, He could have stoned her. Yet He chose not to. His response was not condemnation but grace and encouragement toward repentance.

When we hear the voices of condemnation—whether from others or from ourselves—we can remember these two truths: First, no one else has the right to condemn us. Second, God Himself will never condemn those who are in Christ

Jesus. If we have come to Him in repentance for forgiveness, we are clean before Him. Christ's death means His righteousness is now ours. Second Corinthians 5:21 tells us, "[God] made Him who knew no sin to be sin on our behalf, so that we might become the righteousness of God in Him."

You don't have to be resigned to the life you're living now. When you hear voices of condemnation, stop listening. Counteract these lies with truths from God. If you are dealing with regret from a sin, confess it to God and ask for His forgiveness. Ask Him to help you live in the knowledge that He has set you free.

How would your life change if you were able to live without fearing condemnation from God and others?

RESCUED

WHEN THE JAPANESE BOMBED Manila on the same day they hit Pearl Harbor, my father-in-law, William Rivers, worked for Pan American in Manila. He spent World War II in the Los Baños Japanese prison camp. Several men, including Dad, sneaked out of the camp and gave information to Philippine guerrilla fighters, who passed the intel on to the US military. The air force, army, and navy were able to work together and pull off one of the most spectacular military rescue operations ever executed. Paratroopers hit the camp in the early morning when the Japanese soldiers had stacked their weapons for their daily exercises. Within minutes, twenty-one hundred prisoners close to starvation were free.

Did they rush out of the gates in celebration? No. They stood dazed. They milled around the camp, excited but confused. They talked to the soldiers. *It's so good to see an Ameri-*

can. How's the war going? Some people went back into the barracks to gather the few worthless possessions they had left. No one headed for the gate and freedom.

The camp was behind enemy lines and within Japanese Tiger Division territory. If the American soldiers couldn't get the rescued out, they'd all soon be dead. Time was passing quickly and the prisoners still hung around inside the prison camp. Orders came: set fire to the barracks! Only when the camp was in flames did the freed prisoners board the transport vehicles waiting for them.

Sadly, many people who are rescued and offered freedom do the same thing:

- A rescued girl, a victim of sex-trafficking, returns to her pimp.
- A man spends a lifetime at a job he hates.
- A battered wife refuses to leave her abusive husband.
- A recovering alcoholic stops at a liquor store for just one last six-pack of beer.
- A teenager gives in to peer pressure and lights up a cigarette or inhales vapor.
- A betrayed husband, wife, or friend dwells in bitterness.

We are often more comfortable in captivity than freedom, even when captivity is deadly. We cling to what we know because it is familiar, even though it is not comfortable.

We are all held captive, but most of us never define the prison in which we live. Think of Neo in the movie *The Matrix,* who discovered that what he thought was freedom was really a figment of his imagination. While others preferred

ease and oblivion, he was ready to sacrifice his comfortable
life for genuine liberty. Our souls cry out for liberty. Being
rescued is the first step, as freedom opens the door of whatever cage we're in. But most of us need someone to beckon us
forth, to take our hands and encourage us to follow—someone
on the outside who understands what holds us back in fear.

We're rescued, but it takes courage to step into a life that
will change from the inside out and bring us into the real
world full of the promise that awaits.

You are rescued. Take a step of faith and see what good
news is waiting for you.

Turning Away from Rescue

"I'M NEXT! HOW much?"

Murphy named a high price.

Angel drank the glass of whiskey. Shuddering, she stood as Murphy pulled back her chair. Nothing is ever going to change. *Her heart beat slower and slower as she went up the stairs. By the time she reached the top, she couldn't feel her heart beating at all. She couldn't feel anything.*

I should have stayed with Michael. Why didn't I stay with Michael?

It would never have worked, Angel. Not in a million years.

It did for a while.

Until the world caught up. The world has no mercy, Angel. You know that. It was a desert dream. You just left before he was finished using you. Now you're back where you belong, doing what you were born to do.

What did any of it matter? It was too late to think about what-ifs. It was too late to think about why. It was too late to think about anything.

I t's happened to all of us. We're stuck in a bad situation or habit, and we long to escape. We finally see a way to freedom—but we don't take it. We continue struggling, captive, haunted by missed opportunities, looking back at the escape we passed and asking ourselves, *Why didn't I take the way out?*

Angel had been rescued from the Palace and shown a whole new way of life. Michael was full of kindness and compassion, never harming her or using her. Love was there for her to take, but she turned her back on a life with him, determined to get her gold and set off on her own. Then she discovered the Palace had burned down and the Duchess was gone, and there was no hope of independence. When Murphy suggested she return to prostitution under his roof, she didn't see another option. Numb and hopeless, she agreed. But her heart cried out, *Why didn't I stay with Michael?*

In Romans 7, the apostle Paul wrote with remarkable honesty about the gap between what we want to do and what we actually do.

> I have discovered this principle of life—that when I
> want to do what is right, I inevitably do what is wrong.
> I love God's law with all my heart. But there is another
> power within me that is at war with my mind. This
> power makes me a slave to the sin that is still within me.
> Oh, what a miserable person I am! (verses 21–24, NLT)

If Paul, God's chosen missionary to the Gentiles and the writer of a significant portion of the New Testament, struggled with sin, it's safe to say this is a problem common to every human who ever walked the earth. We know what we should do, yet so often we don't do it. We follow our own desires instead of God's. We live by fear instead of by trust. We turn away from the One who is ready to save us and instead flounder on our own. As Paul so aptly said, there is a war inside us. In this world, we are slaves to our fallen human nature, unable to get free of its clutches.

Then what do we do? Are we stuck forever? Fortunately, Paul's words don't end there.

> Who will free me from this life that is dominated by sin and death? Thank God! The answer is in Jesus Christ our Lord. (verses 24–25, NLT)

Jesus is the *only* solution to the problem of sin. We can't extract ourselves, we can't wash ourselves off, and we can't fix ourselves. We need His help to rescue us and change us. And He does! But sometimes freedom comes a little at a time because we're not ready for more.

Here's the thing: we are changed by our encounters with God. Even when we fall away and go back to captivity, we are not the same people we were before.

Just a few weeks with Michael meant that Angel had lost some of her hardness, her protective veneer. Even though she left him, even though she ended up going back to her old ways, she had changed as a result of experiencing his kindness and genuine love. She could no longer practice prostitution without it costing her. She felt regret over what she had left behind. Though in this moment that change was painful and difficult—being numb made it easier—it meant that God was paving the way for more change. It meant that the next time Angel was faced with a similar dilemma, she might make a different choice.

We all face regret for choices we've made—choices to stay in captivity, to turn away from God, to forget we've been rescued. When you find yourself stuck, telling yourself, *I should have . . .* after you've turned away from being rescued, take heart. Remember that Jesus is the one who will free you. He is capable of using even your failures to work in you.

Philippians 1:6 gives us this promise: "I am certain that God, who began the good work within you, will continue his work until it is finally finished on the day when Christ Jesus returns" (NLT). He will not give up on us when we turn our backs on Him and return to sin. He continues to work in us, changing our hearts little by little until we are finally ready to be set free.

Think of a time when you didn't take an opportunity to be rescued from a bad situation or a sinful habit. What made you turn away from being rescued? Talk to God, thanking Him for His work in your life and asking Him for courage to move forward and accept His rescue.

A God Who Fights for Us

CLOSING DOWN HER emotions, closing down her mind, she went to work.

The door crashed open, and someone yanked the young man away. Angel drew in a sharp breath as she recognized the face of the man above her. "Michael!" She pushed herself up. "Oh, Michael . . ."

Two more men came at him, and he pushed her out of the way just before they hit him. The three went crashing back over a faro table. Chips, cards, and men scattered. Two more entered the fracas.

"Stop it!" she screamed, sure they would kill him. Frantic, she looked for something to use as a weapon to help, but Michael wasn't down long enough. He kicked one man off of him and was on his feet. She stared, mouth agape, as he fought. He stood his ground, punching hard and fast as the other men came at him. Swinging around, he brought one foot up straight into a man's face. She had never seen anyone fight the way he did. He

looked as though he had been doing it all his life instead of plowing furrows and planting corn. He hit square and he hit hard, and those he hit stayed down. After a few minutes, the men weren't so eager to come at him.

Michael stood ready, eyes blazing. "Come on, then," he grated, daring them. "Who else wants to get between me and my wife? Come on!*"*

No one moved.

Have you ever needed someone to fight for you? Angel's relief when Michael burst into the room quickly turned to fear as she saw whom he was up against. Murphy, Max, and many more men in the saloon were ready to fight to keep Angel from leaving with Michael. How could a gentle farmer be a match for these rough barmen and miners? She was stunned when Michael more than held his own, fighting with a fury and zeal she didn't know he possessed. Michael was a peace-loving man, but his righteous anger gave him the power to fight anyone who would attempt to stop him from rescuing his wife.

When we describe God, we often use adjectives such as *kind, loving,* and *good* or perhaps *holy* and *powerful.* All of these are accurate, but they don't present the whole picture. Scripture also portrays God as a warrior.

Back in the days of the Exodus, after God had shown His power through the ten plagues, Pharaoh finally gave his permission for the Israelites to leave Egypt. But shortly after they had started their journey to the wilderness, he changed his mind. Why should he let all his slave labor go free? Pharaoh gathered his army and started out after the Israelites, eventually trapping them by the Red Sea. There was nowhere for them to go. The people panicked, asking Moses why he had brought them into the wilderness to die. But Moses responded,

> Do not fear! Stand by and see the salvation of the LORD which He will accomplish for you today; for the Egyptians whom you have seen today, you will never see them again forever. The LORD will fight for you while you keep silent. (Exodus 14:13–14)

"The LORD will fight for you." You know what happened. The Lord parted the Red Sea, and the people walked through on dry ground. Then, when the soldiers pursued them, the waters closed up and the Egyptian army was destroyed. All the Israelites had to do was walk in faith.

The people sang this song later, praising God for delivering them by His might:

> The LORD is my strength and song,
> And He has become my salvation;
> This is my God, and I will praise Him;
> My father's God, and I will extol Him.
> The LORD is a warrior;
> The LORD is His name. (15:2–3)

The Israelites were rescued despite their fear and complaining. They weren't saved because of anything they had done but because of who God is and what He had planned for them. In the same way, Angel didn't believe she deserved to be rescued. She hadn't done anything to earn Michael's favor— quite the opposite, in fact. She had abandoned him and returned to prostitution. Most husbands would have been happy to see the last of her. Yet Michael not only wanted her back but also went to find her and then fought off anyone who stood in his way.

Can you picture God fighting that way for *you*? He does.

Colossians 1:13–14 tells us, "He has rescued us from the kingdom of darkness and transferred us into the Kingdom of his dear Son, who purchased our freedom and forgave our sins" (NLT). He has brought us out of the darkness and into the light. And when we fall back into old patterns and return to the darkness, our warrior God comes to rescue us again, fighting against anything and anyone that keeps us from coming to Him.

If you made a choice to turn away from God and are stuck in regret, take heart. God has rescued you, and He won't let anyone get between Him and His beloved child.

Visualize the scene where Michael is fighting for Angel. Now imagine that God is fighting even harder for you. What sin or pattern is He fighting that keeps you from coming to Him? How does it change your mindset to know that God considers you worthy of rescue?

Anger and Mercy

KICKING A TURNED table out of his way, Michael strode toward Angel. He didn't look anything like the man she had come to know in the valley. "I told you to keep walking!" He grabbed her arm and swung her toward the doors.

Angel was afraid even to look at him. She was afraid to say a word. She had never seen him like this before, even that one time when he had lost his temper in the barn. This was not the quiet, patient man she thought she knew. This was a stranger bent on vengeance. She remembered Duke lighting his cheroot and broke out in a cold sweat.

Michael wiped blood from his lip. "Make me understand, Angel. Tell me why."

Angel. There was a death knell in the name. "Let me off this wagon."

"You're coming home with me."

"So you can kill me?"

❧

Our response to anger—at least the anger of someone powerful—is often fear.

Angel's first reaction at the sight of Michael had been relief. He had come for her! She didn't understand why, but she was grateful beyond belief. But now, alone with the man who had fought so aggressively for her, she glimpsed the extent of his anger. She had never seen him like this. She judged him by every other man she'd ever known and assumed she would shortly bear the brunt of his wrath. Terrified, she sought to escape.

In our minds, anger is often associated with a lack of control. Angry people do and say things they shouldn't, harming those around them physically or with cutting words. It's frightening to be around them because we don't know what they're going to do next. They might become enraged by a perceived slight or a small frustration that we can't predict. We don't see any upside to anger, and we're uncomfortable with the idea that God ever gets angry or that His anger could be directed at us.

If you, like Angel, have a past that includes abuse, this might be even more frightening. When someone who has rescued us is angry, we feel unsafe. We wonder if it would have been better not to be rescued at all.

But God's anger is different. It can be impassioned, but it is not out of control. Michael told Angel, "I felt like killing you when I walked in that room, but I didn't. I feel like beating sense into you right now, but I won't. And no matter how much it hurts, and no matter how much I feel like hurting you back for what you've done, I'm not going to." Unlike human anger, God's anger never leads to actions He regrets. While we can lose sight of right and wrong in the midst of our emotions, God never does.

God's anger is also different because it is just. It's not triggered by personal slights or hurt pride; instead, He becomes angry at what is evil. Proverbs 6:16–19 gives us a list of things that provoke God's anger:

> There are six things which the LORD hates,
> Yes, seven which are an abomination to Him:
> Haughty eyes, a lying tongue,
> And hands that shed innocent blood,
> A heart that devises wicked plans,
> Feet that run rapidly to evil,
> A false witness who utters lies,
> And one who spreads strife among brothers.

God becomes angry when the people He loves and created are turning away from Him and harming themselves and one another. In Scripture, we often see that the goal of His anger is to effect change. He deeply desires His people to choose what is better.

If we think about it, we can acknowledge that anger is the right reaction to injustice or cruelty. Anger can move us past indifference and fuel us to act so that the situation changes. And God's anger, at least in the history of Israel, communicated to the people how seriously He took sin and ultimately led them back to Him.

Here's another difference between our anger and God's: He doesn't stay angry. While we hold on to our anger long past when it is helpful, He lets go of His as soon as it has accomplished its purpose. His anger is tempered with love.

The prophet Micah warned the people of Judah about God's judgment of sin, but he also reminded them that God was their loving creator and shepherd who would not remain angry with them. This beautiful statement comes toward the end of the book of Micah:

> Who is a God like You, who pardons iniquity
> And passes over the rebellious act of the remnant of His
> > possession?
> He does not retain His anger forever,
> Because He delights in unchanging love.
> He will again have compassion on us;
> He will tread our iniquities under foot.
> Yes, You will cast all their sins
> Into the depths of the sea. (7:18–19)

Unlike some humans who hold grudges and keep the flame of their anger lit at all times, ready to be stoked into a raging fire, God lets His anger pass. His ultimate delight is to show mercy, to forgive and have compassion. This—*forgiveness*—is the ultimate goal.

If you find yourself living in fear that God's anger will be directed at you because of your sin, take heart. Remember that the One who has rescued you is a God who does not stay angry but who delights to show mercy.

When you find yourself frightened by the idea of God's anger, reread Micah 7:18–19 and meditate on the imagery in these verses.

Searching for Freedom

MICHAEL FACED THE road again and was silent for a long time. *"Why did you go back? I just don't get it."*

She closed her eyes, searching for a good enough reason. She could find none and swallowed hard. "To get my gold," she said bleakly. Admitting it aloud made her feel small and hollow.

"What for?"

"I want a little cabin in the woods."

"You've already got one."

She could hardly speak past the lump of pain in her chest. She pressed her hand against it. "I want to be free, Michael. Just once in my whole life. Free!" Her voice broke. She bit her lip and clutched at the side of the wagon seat so hard the wood dug into her hands.

Michael's face softened. The anger vanished but not the hurt, not the sorrow. "You are free. You just don't know it yet."

﹅

How do we define *freedom*?

For Angel, freedom meant independence. For once, she wanted to be in control of her life; she wanted to be the one to make choices about what she would do and when. She longed for a place where she could be alone, where no one would make any demands on her. Complete solitude. Complete autonomy.

We can understand Angel's desire. After a lifetime of abuse, of being controlled by evil people who cared nothing for her and used her for their own selfish gain, she trusted no one. In her mind, the only way to be free was to rely on herself. Most of us have the same desire.

But is that really freedom? Removing other people from our lives doesn't fix the core problem: ourselves.

Living on her own, Angel could have avoided a lot of hurt. But she still would have been stuck with her insecurities and fears, her anger and hardness, her regrets and her wounds. Even without any people imprisoning her, Angel wouldn't have been free. And neither are any of us. Genuine freedom requires God's intervention.

In Galatians 5:1, Paul wrote, "It was for freedom that Christ set us free; therefore keep standing firm and do not be subject again to a yoke of slavery." Christ is the one who sets us free—from the sin and hurts that affect every part of us. Of course, other people contribute to our ensnarement, but our fallen human nature is what keeps us mired in our own fears and prevents us from experiencing all that God has for us.

Once we trust Christ, He sets us free from sin, breaking the power it holds over us and letting us see what life can be like when we follow God and do things His way. And so, Paul exhorts us to remain free—and not to let sin enslave us again.

On the surface, it seems crazy that he would need to tell us this. Why would anyone who has been rescued go back into captivity willingly? Why would we set aside a life of grace to go back to a life of fear and legalism? But that's often what we do. We know the life of fear. Though unpleasant, it's familiar. We've hardened ourselves to it, and we know how to survive it.

The life of grace, on the other hand, is unfamiliar. It strips away our protective shell and transforms us, and that can be uncomfortable. Accepting grace also means we learn to trust our rescuer. Rather than constantly being on our guard, protecting ourselves against being taken advantage of, embracing a life of grace means believing that God is doing what is best for us. God's freedom means we stop fighting for independence and instead embrace surrender to the One who loves us most. When we've only recently been rescued, that can be hard. We're not sure yet that we really want that kind of freedom.

In John 5, we read about a man who had been an invalid for thirty-eight years. Jesus encountered him lying by a pool in Jerusalem, where many disabled people stayed, waiting for the water to bubble up. They believed this stirring of the water was caused by an angel and that the first person who got into the pool after the water moved would be healed.

Jesus's first words to the man were a question: "Do you wish to get well?" (verse 6). What a strange thing to ask. Why wouldn't the man want to get well? Who would choose to live as an invalid, unable to walk or live independently?

The man responded, "Sir, I have no man to put me into the pool when the water is stirred up, but while I am coming, another steps down before me" (verse 7). We don't know the details of this man's life, but we can imagine that in his quest for healing and freedom, he had been trying the same thing over and over for years, with a lot of effort but little hope of success. He was stuck. Did he want healing at all, or had he become comfortable being an object of pity? And even if he wished to be healed, did he desire it enough to try a different tactic and rely on someone else? After all, his response to Jesus was to offer excuses, not to cry out for healing and deliverance.

Maybe Jesus's question—to the man and to us—really comes down to this: "Are you ready to trust that the freedom I give you is best? Are you willing to accept My help and do things My way?"

> Jesus said to him, "Get up, pick up your pallet and
> walk." Immediately the man became well, and picked
> up his pallet and began to walk. (verses 8–9)

If you find yourself doing the same thing over and over and seeing no results, ask yourself how much you really want to change. Are you ready to trust that only your rescuer can bring you genuine freedom?

What does freedom mean to you? Think about what holds you back from embracing the freedom Jesus offers.

Removing the Stains

HE WADED INTO the creek and caught hold of her, yanking her to her feet. Her fists were full of gravel. Her breasts and belly were raw from scrubbing. "What are you doing to yourself?"

"I have to wash. You didn't give me the chance—"

"You've washed enough." He tried to put the jacket around her, and she pulled away.

"I'm not clean yet, Michael. Just go away and leave me alone."

Michael grabbed her roughly. "Will you be finished when you've stripped your skin off? When you've bled? Is that it? Do you think doing this to yourself will make you clean?" He let go of her, afraid he would do her physical harm. "It doesn't work that way," he said through gritted teeth.

She blinked and sat down slowly, the icy water swirling around her waist. "No, I guess not," she said softly.

ngel's realization—and the quiet despair that follows—is heartbreaking.

Michael had rescued her from Pair-a-Dice, fighting for her like an impassioned warrior. But after they arrived home, Angel glimpsed him in the barn, weeping. She understood how deeply she had wounded him through her betrayal. Desperate, she rushed to the cold creek to try to cleanse herself. But no matter how long and how roughly she scrubbed, it wouldn't be enough. She couldn't wash off the stain.

I'm not sure any self-aware human can reach adulthood without having a few moments like this. We are people who make wrong choices that hurt God, others, and ourselves. Sometimes we try to justify our actions or brush aside our wrongdoing as not a big deal. But sooner or later we come face to face with both our own sin and our powerlessness to get rid of it.

When we do, we must choose which way we will turn— toward despair or toward hope.

Angel had felt stained for most of her life. She blamed herself for things that had been done to her, and the weight of that blame led her to make worse choices. She tried to run from her pain and fight against it by not letting herself feel anything or get close to anyone. But now that living with Michael had loosened her defenses, that approach wasn't working anymore. Confronted with the anguish her choices had brought, she reacted with despair, feeling she would never be good enough.

When we feel overwhelming guilt or shame, whether because of our own sin or because of wrongs perpetrated against us, how do we move forward? We can find ourselves doing penance to make up for our mistakes and trying to live perfectly so we don't blow it again. Nothing really helps us feel better. The only one who can get rid of our stains and heal our brokenness is God.

King David wrote Psalm 51 after his sin with Bathsheba. Not only had he committed adultery with a married woman who had then become pregnant, but he also conspired to have her husband killed so that no one would find out. We get the impression David ran from his sin and tried to justify himself—right up until the moment when God sent the prophet Nathan to confront him with a pointed story. When David heard "You are that man!" (2 Samuel 12:7, NLT), his self-justification crumbled, and he was forced to come to terms with what he had done.

In Psalm 51, he wrote these words:

> You do not delight in sacrifice, otherwise I would give it;
> You are not pleased with burnt offering.
> The sacrifices of God are a broken spirit;
> A broken and a contrite heart, O God, You will not
>   despise. (verses 16–17)

David cut to the heart of things. As a wealthy king, he could have afforded scores of sacrifices to atone for his sin. But he rightly understood what was most important to God, and he turned to the Lord in brokenness and repentance. While it is difficult to feel the weight of our past and all the ways we have turned away from God, it's the necessary first step on the path to redemption because it leads us to the second: realizing that God alone can cleanse us.

Titus 3:4–7 says,

> When God our Savior revealed his kindness and love, he
> saved us, not because of the righteous things we had
> done, but because of his mercy. He washed away our
> sins, giving us a new birth and new life through the
> Holy Spirit. He generously poured out the Spirit upon
> us through Jesus Christ our Savior. Because of his grace
> he made us right in his sight and gave us confidence that
> we will inherit eternal life. (NLT)

Doing enough good acts isn't what cleanses us. No matter how heavy our sins or how ugly our past, we're saved because of God's mercy and washed by the Holy Spirit.

If you've been running from the reality of your past and are now starting to feel the weight of it, take heart. Stop running, stop fighting, and acknowledge to yourself and God that you can't make it right on your own. Turn to Him in repentance, knowing He can wash away your stains. He can take your brokenness and turn it into hope.

What have you been hiding or trying to make amends for on your own? Confess it to God and let Him cleanse you completely.

DAY 18

Grabbing the Hand of Rescue

MICHAEL WENT UP *to the hill and sat, forearms resting on his knees. "So what do I do now?" Nothing was the same as it had been. It was as though they both walked side by side, never touching, never talking. She had cut herself wide open and poured her insides out to him the night he brought her home. Now she lay bleeding to death and wouldn't allow the healing to come. She hoped to please him by working like a slave when all he wanted was her love.*

He raked a hand back through his hair and held his head. So, what do I do, Lord? What do I do?

Tend my lamb.

You keep saying that, but I don't know how. I don't know what you mean. I'm not a prophet, Lord. I'm a simple farmer. I'm not up to the task you've set for me. My love hasn't been enough. She's still there in the pit, dying. I reach for her, but she won't take my hand. She'll kill herself trying to earn my love when it's hers already.

ᕙᘯᑯᘰᕗ

Consider this familiar scene in an action movie or TV show: One character hangs from a cliff or a building, barely holding on, while another rushes over and yells, "Grab my hand!" The dangling person uses all of his or her strength to reach up and then is slowly hauled to safety.

But every once in a while, this scene goes in a different direction. The would-be rescuer appears, but the dangling person refuses help—and sometimes even chooses to let go. Why would a person do this? Maybe because he or she doesn't want to accept help from anyone—or doesn't feel worthy of rescue.

Michael was reaching out, trying to help Angel, but she wouldn't grab his hand. Instead, she kept trying to get out of the pit by herself through more work. More penitence, more effort—all while rescue was right in front of her, if she would only reach out and take it.

In Luke 15, we read the familiar story of the prodigal son. After the younger son flouted the traditions of his culture and requested his inheritance in advance, he squandered it all on "wild living" (verse 13, NLT) and ended up starving in another country. Realizing that even the servants in his father's house were fed and clothed, he made his way home, practicing his speech all the way. "I will go home to my father and say, 'Father, I have sinned against both heaven and you, and I am no longer worthy of being called your son. Please take me on as a hired servant'" (verses 18–19, NLT).

The prodigal prepared to make his way back into his father's good graces through hard work. Maybe he thought that when he earned back enough of the money he had lost, his father might consider accepting him again. Whatever his eventual hopes, he decided to lead with the point he thought was most important: he was no longer worthy.

How do we evaluate our own worth? Maybe we base it on our level of productivity, our ratio of good choices to bad, or the absence of any huge sins. Or maybe we base it on how much time we spend praying, reading the Bible, or helping out at church. Whatever our formula, if we come up lacking, we don't trust that God will want to bother with us. We don't feel worthy of His attention and grace.

But the prodigal's father wasn't worried about worthiness. Verse 20 says, "[The prodigal] returned home to his father. And while he was still a long way off, his father saw him coming. Filled with love and compassion, he ran to his son, embraced him, and kissed him" (NLT). The father proceeded to throw a huge welcome-home party, saying, "This son of mine was dead and has now returned to life. He was lost, but now he is found" (verse 24, NLT). We get the impression that if the father had had any idea where the son had been living, he would have searched him out and brought him home a long time ago. Rescue was available to the prodigal even when— maybe especially when—he didn't deserve it.

Rescue is available for all of us, no matter what we think we deserve. All we have to do is grab hold of it.

It takes faith to grab on to someone else and trust that person to pull us out of the pit we're in. If we have to let go of something else to grab hold, it can seem even scarier. What if our rescuer isn't strong enough? Aren't we better off trying to scramble to the top ourselves?

But the One we're asked to grab hold of will never falter. He alone is strong enough to save us.

Psalm 31:1–2 says,

In You, O LORD, I have taken refuge;
Let me never be ashamed;
In Your righteousness deliver me.
Incline Your ear to me, rescue me quickly;
Be to me a rock of strength,
A stronghold to save me.

God can be our rescuer, our rock of refuge, and our strong fortress. He doesn't require us to save ourselves or show that we're worthy. If you feel exhausted from trying to work your way to the top of the cliff, hoping to get back in God's good graces, remember that His rescue is sure and free. What do you have to lose by grabbing His hand?

Imagine yourself dangling from a cliff and you see God's hand being offered to you. You may feel unworthy; maybe you're dangling from the cliff because of your own decisions. But envision yourself grabbing God's hand and being pulled to safety. How does accepting His rescue change your life?

Fearing Judgment

ANGEL CLENCHED HER hands in her lap and kept her head down. What was she doing in a church?

One dark-haired lady in a doe brown bonnet was studying her. Angel's mouth went dry. Did they know already? Did she bear the mark on her forehead?

The preacher was looking straight at her and talking about sin and damnation. Sweat broke out on her, and she felt cold. She was going to be sick.

Everyone stood and started singing. She had never heard Michael sing before. He had a deep, rich voice, and he knew the words without the hymnal offered by the man next to him. He belonged here. He believed all this. Every word of it. She stared forward again and looked into the dark eyes of the preacher. He knows, just like Mama's priest knew.

She had to get out! When they all sat down again, that

preacher would probably point straight at her and ask what she was doing in his church.

Have you ever walked into a room or down the street and felt your bad choices must be obvious to all? *Everyone must know what I've done!* Our guilt over our own mistakes makes us lose perspective, and we feel sure that we're the only ones who haven't led perfect lives. We cringe, ready to face disapproval and condemnation from those who seem to have it all together.

Angel knew how to handle the men who paid to use her body—men whose lives were as checkered with vice and regret as hers was. She didn't know how to face people who lived by a different set of rules. And Christians? They terrified her. If they knew her history, surely they would throw her out of their church in a cloud of righteous indignation.

In our culture of social media, it feels as if everything is on display. We see a few curated, isolated moments from others' lives, and our imaginations fill in the gaps. If their child won a spelling bee, they must be ideal parents in every way. If she got a promotion at work, she must never make a mistake or have a moment of anxiety. What's even more dangerous is when we make these kinds of assumptions about others' relationships with God, supposing that those around us rarely struggle with sin or temptation and are paragons of faith and virtue. We are all too familiar with our own internal failures, and so we compare the messy reality of our lives with the seemingly perfect exterior of others'. And then we expect disapproval and condemnation from anyone who sees us as we really are.

But the truth is that every single person on earth struggles. We're all broken and weary and imperfect. Scripture tells us that everyone has sinned and fallen short of the glory of God (Romans 3:23). Not one person has escaped the crushing failure of sin.

Angel had probably never heard about the Sermon on the Mount, but if she had, she might have been surprised by these words of Jesus: "You have heard that it was said, 'You shall not commit adultery'; but I say to you that everyone who looks at a woman with lust for her has already committed adultery with her in his heart" (Matthew 5:27–28). God isn't concerned with only our behavior. He cares about what goes on in our hearts—our thoughts and attitudes, our jealousy and anger, our pride and fear. And no matter who we are or how good we appear, our hearts are messy and sinful and imperfect.

So why is it human tendency to criticize and judge? Perhaps it makes us feel better about ourselves, at least temporarily. When we're looking at someone else's flaws, our own don't seem so large. But this attitude is dangerous. Jesus warned against it in a vivid illustration from the Sermon on the Mount:

> Do not judge so that you will not be judged. For in the way you judge, you will be judged; and by your standard of measure, it will be measured to you. Why do you look at the speck that is in your brother's eye, but do not notice the log that is in your own eye? (Matthew 7:1–3)

The logs in our eyes make it impossible for us to see others clearly. So why should we waste time condemning others or worrying about their judgment of us? Paul described the way that we as believers should instead treat someone who is struggling with sin:

> Dear brothers and sisters, if another believer is overcome by some sin, you who are godly should gently and humbly help that person back onto the right path. And be careful not to fall into the same temptation yourself. Share each other's burdens, and in this way obey the law of Christ. (Galatians 6:1–2, NLT)

Gently. Humbly. We address sin in another with the goal of helping the person back onto the right path, all the while understanding that no one is beyond this temptation. We share burdens in love. Our goal is rescue, not judgment.

People are imperfect, and this kind of loving response won't always happen. But this is what God calls us to. If you are dealing with temptation or sin and feel afraid of the response you might get from other Christ followers, I hope you will remember this passage and look for at least one person in your community of believers who responds to you with gentleness and humility, pointing you to God's truth and drawing you in rather than pushing you out. After all, if the church isn't for sinners, who is it for?

If you're pulling away from other believers because you're afraid of condemnation, ask God to help you see others more accurately and find supportive relationships.

Learning to Love

ANGEL HAD KNOWN *the questions would come and that making up lies would only tie her into tighter knots. Why not get it over with now, and then the girl would let her be? Maybe if they all knew the truth, they'd winter someplace else. Certainly that woman wouldn't want to sleep in the same bed where a prostitute had slept. "I came to California alone. I met Michael in a brothel in Pair-a-Dice."*

Miriam laughed and then, seeing Angel meant what she'd said, fell silent. "You're serious, aren't you?"

"Yes."

Miriam didn't say anything for a long moment, and Elizabeth closed her eyes again. "You needn't have said anything," Miriam said finally. "Why did you?"

"So you wouldn't have any shocking surprises down the road," Angel said bitterly, her throat tight.

"I'd like to be friends," Miriam said.

Angel glanced up in surprise. "Why would you want to be friends with me?"

Miriam looked surprised. "Because I like you."

❧

When we're mired in our own misery and self-condemnation, it's difficult to think about anyone else.

Angel had never really had a friend except for Lucky—and their relationship was based on their shared status in life. They understood each other because they had so much in common, and since they already knew the worst of each other's past, they didn't have to hide. But Miriam and the rest of the Altmans were a different story.

Angel's years of protecting herself from hurt had formed hard layers around her heart. She didn't trust anyone, and she didn't let anyone in. She decided the best way to push these kind Christian people away for good was to be open about her past—to tell them on her own terms before they could find out and reject her. When Miriam still wanted to be her friend, Angel didn't know how to respond.

The wounds in our past can affect us long after we've been rescued from that past. When we have been hurt by other people, we might see relationships as only potential pain. We lean away from the people who reach out to us, careful not to give them any ammunition with which to wound us more. We begin to think of isolation and independence as ideal.

But this is not what God considers best for us. As messy and painful as relationships can be, they also bring us life. Consider Ecclesiastes 4:9–12:

Two are better than one because they have a good return for their labor. For if either of them falls, the one will lift up his companion. But woe to the one who falls when there is not another to lift him up. Furthermore, if two lie down together they keep warm, but how can one be warm alone? And if one can overpower him who is alone, two can resist him. A cord of three strands is not quickly torn apart.

This passage focuses on practical benefits of relationships—help, warmth, and defense. Yet so much emotion is carried in that third sentence: "But woe to the one who falls when there is not another to lift him up." We might be tempted to believe that if we keep to ourselves, we won't have to help anyone and no one will make demands on us. But isolating ourselves also means that when we're in trouble, we go it alone. That's not what God designed.

We're created to care for others and be cared for by them. From the very beginning, God said, "It is not good for the man to be alone" (Genesis 2:18). He knew that life on this earth would be tough, and we would need others to help us share the load. Romans 12:15 tells us to "rejoice with those who rejoice, and weep with those who weep." When others enter into our sorrow, their compassion makes us feel less alone. When others celebrate with us, our joy expands. And when we care enough to share others' joys and sorrows, our love for them grows and our hearts change.

Loving others takes us outside ourselves. When we don't have to consider anyone else, we can become self-centered, thinking about only what will benefit us. But when we begin to love other people, we care about their well-being. We want the best for them, and that can alter us. Once the Altmans' youngest daughter, Ruthie, took a liking to Angel, Angel had to start responding differently. She didn't mind pushing everyone else away, but she couldn't hurt the feelings of a little child. Loving Ruthie helped Angel start to put aside some of her pride and self-condemnation. She began to consider that she might have something worthwhile to offer.

If you find yourself isolated, withdrawing because of your own insecurities or hurts, remember that God has created us to need other people. Loving others and learning to be loved by them is a gift that can transform us. And that happens best when we put God in the center of our relationships. When Ecclesiastes 4:12 says that a "cord of three strands is not quickly torn apart," it's a reminder that God's presence is what ultimately makes our relationships work. His presence strengthens our relationships, deepens them, and helps them last.

First John 4:12 says, "If we love each other, God lives in us, and his love is brought to full expression in us" (NLT). As we love others, He makes us more like Himself.

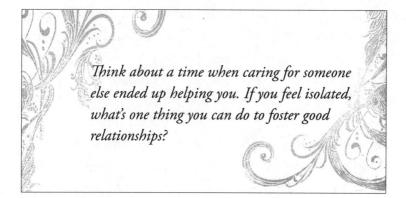

Think about a time when caring for someone else ended up helping you. If you feel isolated, what's one thing you can do to foster good relationships?

Listening to the Right Voice

MIRIAM SET OUT the bowls and glanced at Angel. "Now, tell me what it's all about."

"What?"

"You know what. You and Paul. Was he in love with you before you married Michael?"

Angel gave a sardonic laugh. "Hardly."

Miriam frowned. "He didn't approve."

"Doesn't," Angel said. "With good reason. Don't think too badly of him. He was looking out for Michael." She gave the sifter a last tap and set it aside. "I knew a girl once who received a chunk of amethyst as a gift. It was beautiful. Bright purple crystals. The man told her it came from a stone egg he had cracked open and part of the outer shell was still on it. Gray, ugly, and smooth." She looked at Miriam. "I'm like that, Miriam. Only it's inside out. All the loveliness is here." She touched

her braid and her flawless face. "Inside, it's dark and ugly. Paul saw that."

Tears welled into Miriam's eyes. *"Then he didn't look hard enough."*

❦

D o we let the way others see us determine the way we view ourselves?

Paul was a dark presence in Angel's life, constantly reminding her where she had come from and what she had been. Anytime she started to think she might be able to adapt to this new life with Michael, she imagined Paul there, telling her that she was nothing but garbage and would never change.

Paul reminded her of one of her worst moments, and when she thought about the way she had betrayed Michael, she felt certain that she was exactly as bad as Paul told her she was.

If Paul functioned as the voice of accusation in Angel's life, Miriam became the voice of encouragement. Paul pointed Angel back to her past—what she had been. Miriam pointed her ahead to the future—what she was becoming. Paul looked at Angel through a lens of anger, guilt, and jealousy, while Miriam looked through a lens of love and forgiveness. Paul could see only sin and hardness, but Miriam saw Angel's pain and the ways she was changing. Miriam looked at the heart.

Scripture is clear that our hearts are the highest priority to God. In the Sermon on the Mount, Jesus shows repeatedly that heart attitudes are as important as actions. And in

1 Samuel, we read this truth in a well-known story about God choosing David to be Israel's next king. David was a mighty warrior, but before he was anointed king, he was an inconsequential shepherd—and the youngest of eight sons. When the prophet Samuel received word from God that one of Jesse's sons was to be the next king, he asked Jesse to bring the young men in front of him. The oldest was tall and handsome, and Samuel thought surely he was the one God had chosen. But God told Samuel to look again. "God sees not as man sees, for man looks at the outward appearance, but the Lord looks at the heart" (1 Samuel 16:7). The Lord was not concerned with how David looked or what he had accomplished already. What was most important was David's attitude toward God and how God would be able to use him in the future.

We often feel unfairly evaluated, don't we? People make judgments about us based on our appearance, our finances, our work successes, our friendships, our personalities—all without having any idea what is happening on the inside. Sometimes people condemn us without even giving us a chance. We feel unseen, unknown. So it's a gift when we have someone in our lives who sees past the external and looks at our hearts. It's even more of a gift when that person reminds us who we really are on the inside.

All of us in this world will have to deal with people like Paul—people who disapprove of us and won't let us live down things we did in the past. If you feel as if you can't get away from others' negative opinions of you and those negative opinions are affecting the way you think of yourself, hold on to the truth from 1 John 3: "See how very much our Father loves us, for he calls us his children, and that is what we are!" (verse 1, NLT). If you are a follower of Christ, you are a child of God. You have been rescued. God is transforming you. *That* is what is in your heart.

We need to learn to listen to the right voices, the Miriams in our lives, who will encourage us with the truth of who we are. And most of all, we need to learn to listen to the voice of Jesus. John 10:27 says, "My sheep hear My voice, and I know them, and they follow Me." When we learn to identify and listen to the voice of our shepherd, we will never forget we are rescued people.

Who is a Miriam in your life? Identify one or two people who encourage you, point you toward God, and remind you who you really are. Then take time this week to connect with them.

Nothing Can Separate Us

ANGEL HAD SWORN she would never love anyone, and now it was happening in spite of her. It stirred and grew against her will, pushing its way through the darkness of her mind to the surface. Like a seedling seeking the light of the spring sun, it came on. Miriam, little Ruth, Elizabeth. And now Michael. Every time she looked at him, he pierced her heart. She wanted to crush the new feelings, but still they came, slowly finding their way.

Duke was right. It was insidious. It was a trap. It grew like ivy, forcing its way into the smallest cracks of her defenses, and eventually it would rip her apart. If she let it. If she didn't kill it now.

There's still a way out, *came the dark voice, counseling her.* **Tell him the worst of what you've done. Tell him about your father. That'll poison it. That will stop the pain growing inside you.**

So she decided to confess everything. Once Michael knew

everything, it would be finished. The truth would drive a wedge
in so deep between them, she would be safe forever.

⌘

When we push people away with our hurtful words and actions, sometimes they push back. Sometimes they give up on us. But when we try to push God away, He remains faithful.

Afraid of the emotional ties she was developing with the Altmans and Michael, Angel decided the only escape was to kill those feelings. She would tell Michael the worst things she had ever done, and he would be disgusted and reject her. He would no longer love her, and she would be safe.

Angel judged Michael by all the people she'd ever known— people who had abandoned her at the first sign of disappointment or trouble, or maybe even sooner. But things didn't work out the way she expected. Yes, Michael was wounded. He grieved because of what she'd done and the knowledge that she couldn't have children. He prayed to God in distress, not sure why this was happening. But his love did not waver. He listened to Angel, mourned with her, and comforted her. And then, responding to a comment Angel had made about her childhood, he gave her a gift by building her a set of wind chimes.

We can't judge God by what we know of humans. He doesn't work that way. His grace surprises us, even when we've walked with Him for years. Even when we've seen it before. When we're in the pit of despair, knee-deep in our own sin or hurt, His grace is greater than we can imagine.

Paul laid this out in Romans 5:

> When we were utterly helpless, Christ came at just the
> right time and died for us sinners. Now, most people
> would not be willing to die for an upright person,
> though someone might perhaps be willing to die for a
> person who is especially good. But God showed his
> great love for us by sending Christ to die for us while we
> were still sinners. (verses 6–8, NLT)

God doesn't require us to clean up before we approach
Him. He didn't command us to shape up before He reluc-
tantly agreed to die on our behalf. No. He chose to die for us
while we were still mired in our sin, with no way to get out.
He chooses to love us when we still sin today. He chooses to
love us when we turn our backs on Him and live as if He
doesn't exist, even as He calls us to return.

Nothing can keep us from God's love. Romans 8:38–39
communicates this beautifully:

> I am convinced that neither death, nor life, nor angels,
> nor principalities, nor things present, nor things to
> come, nor powers, nor height, nor depth, nor any other
> created thing, will be able to separate us from the love of
> God, which is in Christ Jesus our Lord.

What hardships could we add to this passage? Each of us
fears being separated from God's love for a certain reason.
What is yours? A particular failure? Pride? A sin you just can't
seem to overcome? Tough financial circumstances or conflict-

ridden family relationships? Bad habits? Lack of time spent praying or studying the Bible? None of these can separate us from the love of God that is in Christ Jesus our Lord. Nothing can.

We can't scare God away with our sins or push Him away with our anger. We can't run away from Him. His love is bigger than that.

Psalm 139 talks about God's constant presence:

Where can I go from Your Spirit?
Or where can I flee from Your presence?
If I ascend to heaven, You are there;
If I make my bed in Sheol, behold, You are there.
If I take the wings of the dawn,
If I dwell in the remotest part of the sea,
Even there Your hand will lead me,
And Your right hand will lay hold of me. (verses 7–10)

For someone who has a history of abuse, these verses might sound menacing at first. We can't get away from God? But then we realize that they are simply stating the truth: God is always with us because He is everywhere. There's nowhere we can go to escape from Him—and that's a good thing because His intentions for us are the very best. Verse 10 makes clear what God does while He's close by: He guides us in His wisdom and holds us by the hand. We don't need to fear. God offers love.

If you find yourself trying to push God away, remember that He will always be faithful to you. Nothing can keep you apart from His love.

Deep down, what do you fear can separate you from God? Write down Romans 8:38–39, including your additional fears, and put it somewhere you will see it each day.

REDEEMED

To BE REDEEMED IS to have our freedom purchased by someone else, someone who was willing to pay the price for our freedom, no matter the cost.

What would make someone do that?

Love, but not love as we know it. A love beyond comprehension yet craved and longed for from the womb. The kind of love that has no limits but has the power to change the mind, heart, and soul of a person. A love that's impossible to maintain without a power greater than ourselves. Like the character of Michael in *Redeeming Love*. He loves God more than anyone and is therefore willing and able to love Angel in the same all-consuming, passionate way Jesus first loved him.

It took thirty-seven years for me to surrender to God's love. Thirty-plus years have gone by since then, and I still find myself in awe of Him, still discovering how pale my understanding is of the height, depth, and width of the love that

God has for me—and for you. We are human. We can see only parts, not the whole.

Being redeemed releases us from blame, from debt. Spiritually, we are free from the consequences of every bad thing we've ever done, every evil thought we've held, every cruel, untrue, unkind, nasty word we've said. No, it's not fair. It's not just. It's not deserved. That's why it's called God's grace.

Before accepting God's gift of grace, when I looked back over my life, I saw a garbage heap of things I wish I'd never done, never thought, or never said. Stripped of justifications, rationalizations, I found myself staring at the truth. I was a mess, though I felt far worse than that simple word suggests. But once I accepted God's gift of grace, I felt blessed and thankful. Jesus suffered the worst of human brutality and died to redeem me—not just from what I had done in the past but from what I would do in the future when I would undoubtedly stumble, trip, and fall despite my best efforts to follow Him. And He would be there, ready and able to help me up again.

Most of us want to deal with our own messes in our own way and in our own time. Many times that means denying we are a mess, pursuing our own paths, and forgetting time comes to an end, often when we least expect it. Some know we're in the hole, far down, close to the pit, deep in debt (and I'm not talking money). When I was, I longed for a different life. A reboot. A new chance. The amazing thing is, I got it. And so can you.

Rescue opens the prison door. Redemption takes your hand and brings you into freedom.

Learning What Love Is

"LOVE CLEANSES, BELOVED. It doesn't beat you down. It doesn't cast blame." Michael kissed her again, wishing he had the right words to say what he felt. Words would never be enough to show her what he meant. *"My love isn't a weapon. It's a lifeline. Reach out and take hold, and don't let go."*

When he drew her into his arms this time, she didn't struggle. When she put her arms around him, he sighed, the stress of the past weeks dissolving. "This feels good, doesn't it? And right."

"I couldn't stop thinking about you," she said miserably, pressing closer, inhaling the sweet scent of his body. She had missed this feeling of safety that only came when she was with him. He was so determined to have her. Well, why not let him? Wasn't it what she wanted? To belong to him. To stay with him forever. Wasn't this what she had longed for every moment since she had left him?

"You make me hope, Michael. I don't know if that's good or not."

"It's good," he said, holding her close and rejoicing at her admission. *It was a beginning.*

⁂

Why does genuine love look like?
        Angel's idea of love was warped by what she had observed in her mother's life. In Angel's mind, love weakened you. When you loved someone, you were at that person's mercy. If loved ones could hurt you simply by withdrawing their presence or affection, they could utterly crush you by walking out of your life. Angel had watched her mother become so dependent on Alex that once he left, she lost all will to live. So when she felt herself falling in love with Michael, she did the only thing she could think of—she ran away.

But Michael came after her. He tried to convince her that the love she felt for him was good and that he would never use her need for him against her. His love was categorically different than the twisted love she had observed in her parents' relationship because it grew out of his love for God, not out of his selfishness.

We all carry distorted views of love. We glean them from movies and TV shows, celebrity news, magazines and books, and our experiences. Some are positive and idealistic:

- "Love is an overwhelming feeling that makes life worthwhile."

- "Romantic love completes your life."
- "Love is perfect and easy when it's shared with the one right person."

Others are more negative:

- "Love doesn't last."
- "Love is about getting what you want."
- "Love ties you down."

Not surprisingly, the way we think about romantic love affects the way we think about God's love. If we are convinced that love never lasts, we'll doubt the steadfastness of God's. If we think romantic love is the pinnacle of human existence, we might not understand the importance of God's. But His faithful love changes everything.

Love is a recurring theme in the apostle John's epistles. In 1 John 4, he wrote about how God's love changes us:

> We know how much God loves us, and we have put our trust in his love.
>
> God is love, and all who live in love live in God, and God lives in them. And as we live in God, our love grows more perfect. So we will not be afraid on the day of judgment, but we can face him with confidence because we live like Jesus here in this world.
>
> Such love has no fear, because perfect love expels all fear. If we are afraid, it is for fear of punishment, and this shows that we have not fully experienced his perfect love. (verses 16–18, NLT)

God *is* love, and the more we know Him and trust Him, the more we begin to grasp His nature. And as we understand His love more fully, we lose our fear. Because we know God is faithful, we don't fear He will leave us. Because we know God is forgiving, we don't fear He will hold our sins against us. Because we know God is good, we don't fear He will harm us. "Perfect love expels all fear," and we can be secure in His love.

In 1 Corinthians 13, Paul described godly love:

> Love is patient, love is kind and is not jealous; love does not brag and is not arrogant, does not act unbecomingly; it does not seek its own, is not provoked, does not take into account a wrong suffered, does not rejoice in unrighteousness, but rejoices with the truth; bears all things, believes all things, hopes all things, endures all things.
>
> Love never fails. (verses 4–8)

Even the kindest people will fail at expressing this sort of love, but God never will. Human love is ultimately about getting what we want and need. But God doesn't need anything from us. He loves us with no expectation of gaining anything by it; He does not "seek [His] own." His love is selfless and perfect. It reflects who He is.

The One who redeemed us—who calls us into freedom—loves us perfectly. If you find yourself resisting God's love because of fear or distrust that you've developed as a result of failed human relationships, remember that there is no risk in accepting His love because His love is perfect. It never fails.

Reread 1 John 4:16–18, and think about what it means for perfect love to drive out fear. In what ways are you afraid of God or do you doubt His faithfulness? Confess those to Him, and ask Him to help you grasp His perfect love for you.

Giver of Good Gifts

"WHAT'S WRONG?" HE asked, nuzzling her neck. "Something's been eating at you all evening. Did Miriam or Ruth say something to upset you?"

"Not on purpose. It's just that I'm so happy," she said, her voice shaking. "I can't get over feeling that I don't deserve this."

"And you think I do?" He tugged her braid lightly. "Don't you see? Neither of us deserves this. It's got nothing to do with whether we do or not. Every blessing comes down from the Father, not in payment for good done, but as a gift."

Our culture is obsessed with getting what we deserve. We demand our rights, and we'll fight for what we think we're owed. And yet sometimes, after we've succeeded in getting what we clamored for, a quiet voice in our minds tells us, *You don't deserve this. It won't last.* Maybe we fight so hard because we're always afraid what we have will be taken away.

Angel didn't think she had a right to be happy. After spending years in horrible circumstances, she had internalized the idea that she had gotten exactly what she deserved. If life had been hard, it must be because she wasn't worthy of anything better. When she finally found herself rescued from her old life and happy in her new one, she wasn't sure what to think. Surely it was all a mistake. She didn't deserve anything good, so her happiness would be snatched away from her all too soon.

But as Michael tried to explain, the wonderful things we experience in life are not earned. They're not prizes we snag because we're righteous enough or rewards doled out little by little to keep us doing the right thing. Instead, they're free gifts from our good God.

James 1:17 reiterates this: "Every good thing given and every perfect gift is from above, coming down from the Father of lights, with whom there is no variation or shifting shadow."

Our health. Our families. The beauty of nature. The Bible. Music. Art. Our bodies. All these are gifts from God, given freely to those He loves.

When we look at the world around us, we see abundance everywhere. God did not create a utilitarian world that gives humans just enough to survive. He created a world with an astounding variety of plants and animals—seemingly not for a practical purpose but primarily for His and our pleasure. He created color and sunshine and beauty. He gave us the ability to work and imagine and create. And He gave us the ability to love and be loved, to enjoy the gift of relationships with others and especially with Him.

When we think about being redeemed, we might have a picture of God leading us out of the bad things that held us captive. But do we think much about what He is leading us *into*? Redemption is not just the absence of slavery and sin. God is bringing us into freedom. Into joy and beauty. Into love, both human and divine.

In Psalm 103, David assembled a list of many of God's blessings:

> Bless the LORD, O my soul,
> And all that is within me, bless His holy name.
> Bless the LORD, O my soul,
> And forget none of His benefits;
> Who pardons all your iniquities,
> Who heals all your diseases;
> Who redeems your life from the pit,
> Who crowns you with lovingkindness and compassion;
> Who satisfies your years with good things,
> So that your youth is renewed like the eagle. (verses 1–5)

God gives us forgiveness. Physical and emotional healing. Redemption. Love and compassion. He satisfies our desires and renews our youth. He blesses us with good gifts—not because He has to or because we have earned them through our good works but because we are His children and He loves us.

If we are unable to earn God's gifts through our actions,

we don't lose them by our actions either. God isn't standing by, ready to snatch away our blessings the moment we step out of line. He is a loving Father who gives good gifts.

In Matthew 7:9–11, Jesus underscored this truth:

> You parents—if your children ask for a loaf of bread, do you give them a stone instead? Or if they ask for a fish, do you give them a snake? Of course not! So if you sinful people know how to give good gifts to your children, how much more will your heavenly Father give good gifts to those who ask him. (NLT)

If you find yourself constantly bracing for trouble and waiting for the things dear to your heart to be taken away, remember that your heavenly Father gives good gifts because of who He is, not because of who we are. We don't have to fear that His generosity will come to an end. The One who has redeemed us is faithful.

Spend some time looking at and listening to the world around you. What are some of the gifts God has given you? What might they tell you about His character?

Relinquishing Idols

MICHAEL LOVED HER now, *and that was all that mattered to her. He made her life meaningful and filled it with new and wondrous things. Though life was hard work from dawn to dusk, he somehow made it exciting. He opened her mind to things she hadn't noticed before. And a quiet voice in her head said over and over,* **Come forth, beloved.**

Come forth from what?

She couldn't get enough of Michael. He filled her mind and heart. He was her life. He awakened her before dawn with kisses, and they lay in the quiet darkness, listening to the symphony of crickets and bullfrogs and the wind chimes. Her body trembled at his touch and sang at his possession. Every moment of every day with him was precious to her.

Michael saw God in everything. He saw him in the wind and the rain and the earth. He saw him in the crops that were

growing. He saw God in the nature of the animals that inhab-
ited their land. He saw him in the flames of their evening fire.
Angel only saw Michael and worshiped him.

What is most important to us? What do we value above all else?

For Angel, it was Michael. Once she stopped resisting and allowed herself to love him, she fell hard. Michael had rescued her from degradation and shown her a new life full of possibilities. Married to him, Angel began to understand what selfless love really was. She basked in the warmth and joy that come when two people trust each other, and she discovered the satisfaction that results from hard work. The more she opened up to Michael and this new life, the more she loved the one who had made it possible. Michael became the center of her life and her reason for living.

She began to make him an idol.

When we hear the word *idol,* we might think of the golden calf or some other pagan statue worshiped back in ancient times. It might seem quaint—hardly the kind of thing that applies to us today. But the truth is that anything we love more than God or consider more important than Him can become an idol.

What's your idol? Maybe you, like Angel, make a relationship your idol. Whether it's a spouse, a parent, or a child, you can't imagine life going on without that person. Or maybe your idol is money—either its presence or its lack. Perhaps the security of your retirement funds is the most important thing in your life, or perhaps your desire for more money has become the driving force behind your choices. Status or reputation can become idols, too, if they take first place in our hearts.

How can we recognize whether we have made an idol of something? Imagine life without it or try to go without it for a day or two and see what kind of anxieties or emotions this evokes. We should consider carefully, what do we think we can't live without having?

The truth is, while the things we cling to and place at the center of our lives are deeply important, they often aren't the most crucial. When it comes down to reality, the only thing we can't live without is God.

Make no mistake, losing someone we love is an undeniable tragedy and a loss that brings incomparable grief. So are many other circumstances we endure or watch loved ones face. Yet, with God by our side, our lives go on—differently, painfully, imperfectly—but with hope in eternal life and God's plan. If the stock market crashed and our retirement accounts were emptied, our life plans would change drastically and we might struggle mentally and physically, but God would be with us and we could forge a way forward. If we lost a job or found our reputation in tatters, it would be immensely painful—yet God would still be with us and His opinion of us would remain unchanged.

But if we didn't have God? If He wasn't here to help us and guide us? We wouldn't last a minute. He sustains all creation with His powerful hand. He is the Most High, the only One who is worthy of our worship.

The beginning of the Ten Commandments, as recorded in Exodus 20, addresses the idolatry question head-on:

> I am the LORD your God, who brought you out of the land of Egypt, out of the house of slavery.
> You shall have no other gods before Me.
> You shall not make for yourself an idol. (verses 2–4)

One reason we need to avoid idols is because when we worship them, we take our gaze away from the One who deserves worship. We are forgetting who God really is and setting our hopes and security on something far less—something that can't help us at all. And that is deeply harmful. Not only does it move us further away from a relationship with the one true God, but it also leads us to cynicism. When we put our hope in something fallible and it does indeed fail, we give up.

Angel had confused her rescuer with her redeemer. Michael had rescued her from Pair-a-Dice and brought her safely to this new life, but he wasn't the one who could redeem her and genuinely make her new. Michael could point her to God, but he wasn't God. As wonderful as Michael was, he might someday disappoint her or fail her—but God never would.

We're not called to avoid idolatry because God wants all the attention. It's because He wants what is best for us. He doesn't want us to experience the hurt that comes from putting the wrong thing at the center of our lives or from leaning on a support that isn't strong enough to hold us up. He wants us to know Him more fully and understand who He is: the one true God who is faithful from everlasting to everlasting.

When we see Him as He is, we'll realize that He stands alone. Revelation 5:12 tells us, "Worthy is the Lamb that was slain to receive power and riches and wisdom and might and honor and glory and blessing." Nothing else deserves our worship.

If you find yourself holding more tightly to anything other than to God, remember that only He is worthy of being at the center of our lives. When we keep Him there, everything else will fall into its rightful place.

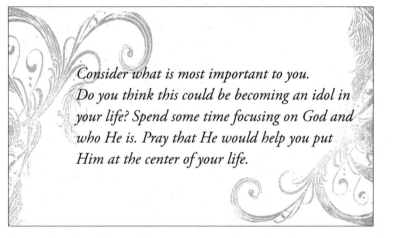

Consider what is most important to you. Do you think this could be becoming an idol in your life? Spend some time focusing on God and who He is. Pray that He would help you put Him at the center of your life.

Satisfying Our Longing

ANGEL STOOD BY *the bed for a long moment. Elizabeth was curled on her side, her knees drawn up and her hand resting protectively on her unborn child. An embrace. Angel looked down at her own flat stomach and spread her hands there. Her eyes burned, and she bit her lip. Dropping her hands to her sides, she turned away and saw Miriam standing in the doorway.*

Miriam smiled wistfully. "I've wondered myself what it would be like. It's a woman's reason for being, isn't it? Our divine privilege: to bring new life into the world and nurture it." She smiled at Angel. "Sometimes I can hardly wait."

Angel saw the tears Miriam tried to hide. After all, what good was divine privilege to a virgin girl?

Or a barren woman.

D o you have a longing you fear will never be fulfilled?
Angel had grown to love the Altman family—yet seeing their caring interactions had set off a deep desire in her for the family she'd never had. Now, watching Elizabeth go through the stages of pregnancy had evoked even deeper longings for the babies Angel was unable to bear. Because of Duke's actions, she and Michael would miss out on this enormous part of life, this blessing from God that was seen as the pinnacle of a woman's existence during this time period. It didn't seem fair.

Our desires can be so strong that they're almost physical. We might even think there's no way to go on with life if we don't attain what we're longing for. What is it for you? Perhaps you're dealing with the pain of infertility and you desperately want a child. Perhaps you are lonely and longing for good friends. Maybe you are single and want so much to get married, but it doesn't look like that will happen and you feel as if life is passing you by. Or maybe you're longing for a new job, a turnaround in a wayward child or spouse, or an improvement in your financial situation. Whatever we're longing for can consume our thoughts. We develop tunnel vision and are unable to see past the thing we want so much.

It's a hard place to be. Our hopes might rise, only to be dashed—time and time again. We feel as if there's no escape, and we wonder why God won't answer. A thought echoes in our minds: *I don't want my life to be this way!* We want the life we've envisioned, not the one we see unfolding before us. We can become angry and bitter.

If you're in this place, be encouraged with the truth that God knows your longings. He "hears your sighs and counts your tears," as an old hymn says.* In Psalm 38:8–9, the psalmist wrote, "I am exhausted and completely crushed. My groans come from an anguished heart. You know what I long for, Lord; you hear my every sigh" (NLT). He knows, and He cares.

When we're longing for a reality that doesn't come, eventually we have to accept that what we want is not what God is giving us, at least for the time being. Sometimes the longing remains, and we live in a kind of limbo, not knowing what the ultimate outcome will be. We try to trust in God's goodness while we wait for His answer. But in the midst of this tension, God helps us by lining up our desires with His.

Psalm 37:4–7 says:

Delight yourself in the LORD;
And He will give you the desires of your heart.
Commit your way to the LORD,
Trust also in Him, and He will do it.
He will bring forth your righteousness as the light
And your judgment as the noonday.

Rest in the LORD and wait patiently for Him.

Some people have used this passage as a divine guarantee— that if we love the Lord enough, He'll give us everything we want. But I don't think that's what David is saying. Instead, I think the key is in the first line: "Delight yourself in the LORD." We're called to seek Him and know Him. When God

---

* Paul Gerhardt, "Give to the Winds Your Fears," 1656, trans. by John Wesley, 1739, public domain.

Himself is our greatest delight, His presence is what we long for most. He becomes our deepest desire. That doesn't mean that we no longer care about our other longings, but it does mean that we view them through a different lens.

At the beginning of Psalm 42, David talked about his longing for God with an insightful metaphor:

> As the deer longs for streams of water,
>   so I long for you, O God.
> I thirst for God, the living God. (verses 1–2, NLT)

When we thirst for God, we know that thirst can be quenched. God doesn't hide from us; Scripture tells us that when we seek Him, we will find Him. We will be satisfied. And when we draw close to Him, we trust Him more. We know that He is with us, that He will help us bear our longings, and that He will not let us miss out on His perfect plan. Psalm 103:5 tells us that He "satisfies your desires with good things" (NIV).

If you worry life is passing you by because your days aren't unfolding the way you desire, take heart. While marriage and family and smooth life circumstances are wonderful, they are not our reason for being. Our purpose is to know Christ and live in His redemption. He is to be our greatest longing. And He will satisfy us with good things.

Reread Psalm 37:4–7 and meditate on what it means to delight in the Lord.

DAY 27

Sacrificial Love

THE ROSE BUSHES *Michael had brought home to Angel bloomed early. She touched the scarlet buds and thought of her mother. She was so much like Mae. She was good for growing flowers, looking pretty, and giving a man pleasure. Beyond that, what good was she?*

Michael should have children. He *wants* children.

She knew on Christmas night what she should do, but it was unbearable to even think of leaving him, of living without him. She wanted to stay here and forget the look in his eyes when he held Benjamin. She wanted to cling to him and bask in the happiness he gave her.

It was that very selfishness that made her realize she didn't deserve him.

Michael had given her everything. She had been empty, and he had filled her to overflowing with his love. She had betrayed him, and he had taken her back and forgiven her. He had sac-

rificed pride to love her. How could she discard his needs after that? How could she live with herself knowing that she had ignored the desires of his heart? What of Michael? What was best for him?

⸎

Hat are we willing to give up for someone else?
Seeing Michael hold baby Benjamin Michael, his namesake, became a turning point for Angel. She no longer could ignore what she had been feeling for some time—that she was holding Michael back from the life he should have. Michael wanted children, and she could see what a caring father he would be. But her barrenness was preventing him from fulfilling that dream. She also knew him well enough to be sure that he would never leave her because she couldn't give him children.

Every time in the past that Angel had run away, she had done it for herself. She ran because she wanted her gold and independence, because she couldn't adapt to a new life, or because she was simply afraid of love. But this time was different. She was running away for Michael's sake. He had rescued her, shown her a new way of life, and loved her when she was most unlovable. His love had transformed her and opened up a new world. But what had she ever given him? When she thought about his needs, she came to one conclusion: she had to leave. If she did, he might marry Miriam and have the family Angel was sure God had planned for him.

Our culture often thinks of romantic love as a commodity

that gives us things—positive feelings, a sense of security, physical fulfillment. It's not uncommon for people to move on from relationships that no longer provide them with what they think they need. But when we love the way God does, we think less about what we can get and more about what we can offer.

In Philippians 2, the apostle Paul challenged the church to have the selfless attitude Christ did:

> Do nothing from selfishness or empty conceit, but with humility of mind regard one another as more important than yourselves; do not merely look out for your own personal interests, but also for the interests of others. Have this attitude in yourselves which was also in Christ Jesus, who, although He existed in the form of God, did not regard equality with God a thing to be grasped, but emptied Himself, taking the form of a bond-servant, and being made in the likeness of men. Being found in appearance as a man, He humbled Himself by becoming obedient to the point of death, even death on a cross. (verses 3–8)

It's impossible to give more than Jesus did. He "gave up his divine privileges" in coming to earth as a human (verse 7, NLT). Theologians over the centuries have had different ideas about what exactly that means, but the bottom line is that He let go of what He had for our sakes. He left the perfection of heaven and entered into our messy, oftentimes ugly existence here on earth. Then He gave up His very life for us, bearing the weight of all our sins and allowing Himself to be separated from the Father, receiving nothing in return. His selflessness gave us a way to be reconciled to God.

This is the attitude Paul tells us to have. One that cares not just for ourselves but also—or perhaps even more—about others. One that lets go of pride and reputation and getting and instead takes the opportunity to share generously. One that gives so completely and so thoroughly that nothing is left out.

Self-focus is part of our human nature. It naturally colors every decision we make. We're geared to think of ourselves first, so it takes a deliberate choice to turn that upside down and put our needs second. We're called to think foremost about the well-being of others, to consider what is best for them and pursue it, even if it is not best for us.

Angel's love for Michael compelled her to act. The very love she had experienced from him changed her. His selflessness in caring for her at great cost to himself allowed her to experience unconditional, other-focused love. Slowly, she came to love him that way too. Once she knew she was loved fully and completely, despite who she was or how she acted, she relaxed her grip on what she thought she should get and instead thought about those around her.

This isn't an attitude we manufacture. Christ's love effects this same transformation in us. The more we understand how deeply and selflessly He loves us, the more we are able to forget about ourselves because we're already taken care of. We're able to love others more selflessly. Paul wrote in 2 Corinthians 5:14 that "Christ's love compels us" (NIV). God's love is the fuel for our own.

If you're stuck in relationships, struggling to act in a self-less way toward others, the solution isn't just to will yourself to greater selflessness. Instead, fix your eyes on Jesus. Reflect on His love and His choices, and remember that you are already cared for and redeemed. Let His love transform yours.

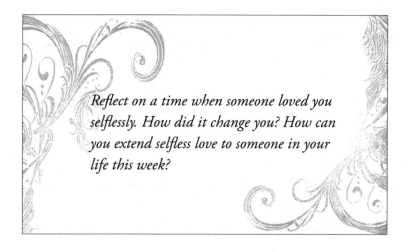

Reflect on a time when someone loved you selflessly. How did it change you? How can you extend selfless love to someone in your life this week?

When Bargaining Doesn't Work

HE CLOSED HIS eyes against the fear uncurling in the pit of his stomach. *I love her, Lord. I can't give her up.*

Michael, beloved. Would you have her hang on her cross forever?

Michael let out a shuddering sigh. When she lifted her face, he saw something in it that made him want to weep. She loved him. She really loved him. And yet, there was something else in her moonlit face. A haunting sadness he couldn't take away, an emptiness he could never fill. He remembered her anguished words on the night Benjamin was born. "I wish I was whole!" He couldn't make her so.

Lifting her, he held her cradled in his arms. She put her arm around his neck and kissed him. He closed his eyes. Lord, if I give her up to you now, will you ever give her back to me?

No answer came.

Lord, please!
The wind stirred softly, but there was only silence.

Haven't we all tried to bargain with God? *If I do this for You, will You give me what I want?*

Michael knew Angel was preparing to leave, and he didn't think he could face it again. When he sensed God telling him to let her go, he wanted only to hold more tightly. Why would God ask him to give up someone he loved so much?

It's as if Michael was keeping one hand on Angel, waiting to release his grip until God promised she would return to him. He wanted assurance, but God was asking him to act without it—to let Angel go without knowing what the end result would be.

On some level, we wish we could successfully bargain with God and guarantee a certain outcome. Who wouldn't want to live with the certainty that the cancer would be healed, the accident avoided, the mistake erased—as long as we held up our end of the deal and did what we promised?

But on another level, is that really what we desire? Should circumstances ultimately be dependent on what we do? Do we want a God who can be manipulated into giving us—and everyone else—a certain outcome if we commit to doing something big enough to persuade Him?

This way of thinking goes back millennia, and it often leads down a terrible road. If you offer something to God and He doesn't seem to answer, isn't the next logical step to offer more? Ancient cultures that incorporated human sacrifice into their religions were surely motivated by this mindset, thinking that they could gain favor with their gods by offering them something as precious as a person's life.

This isn't far from what many people do today—constantly promising God acts of service or generosity in return for favorable outcomes. Some of us prefer living this way because it gives us the illusion of being in control. But imagine carrying this burden year in and year out, always weighing what a particular outcome is worth and what you're willing to give up for it. How exhausting. And living with this worldview puts the burden squarely on us to determine what we want, what we need, and what is best.

That's way beyond our pay grade. We are not wise enough to consider all the ramifications of our decisions. Don't we really want a God who knows what is best for us and does it, even when we don't like it? And beyond that, don't we need a God who is wise enough to do what is best for the whole world?

That's exactly the kind of God we have! Proverbs 2:6 reminds us of His wisdom: "The LORD gives wisdom; from His mouth come knowledge and understanding." The apostle Paul told us that "in [Christ] lie hidden all the treasures of wisdom and knowledge" (Colossians 2:3, NLT). And he told us about God's ultimate goal for our benefit: "This is good and pleases God our Savior, who wants everyone to be saved and to understand the truth" (1 Timothy 2:3–4, NLT). He wants us to receive His salvation and to know Him, which is the best outcome we can imagine.

But believing that God is like this—especially in those moments when we have to let go of something we love or when we're unsure that the outcome we want will ever come to pass—

requires trusting in God's wisdom as well as in His goodness. It requires us to look at the long term rather than the short term.

In Matthew 16:24–25, Jesus told His disciples, "If anyone wishes to come after Me, he must deny himself, and take up his cross and follow Me. For whoever wishes to save his life will lose it; but whoever loses his life for My sake will find it."

We spend so much time and effort trying to save our lives—trying to avoid pain or difficulty, trying to make things go the way we want. How would it feel to let go of that? To surrender ourselves to God and let Him make the choices, trusting that He is good? What would it be like to deny ourselves and lose our lives for His sake?

Surrendering to God doesn't mean we welcome all the short-term outcomes, but I think one day we'll realize they were worth the pain. We see this throughout Scripture—in the lives of Joseph, Moses, and Esther, to name just a few, who all went through challenging personal circumstances but ended up playing significant parts in God's plan to save His people. When we trust that God knows what He is doing, we find freedom in surrendering to Him and knowing we're part of His greater plan.

If you find yourself wanting to bargain with God, remember the kind of God He is. Our Redeemer is wise and good. Trust Him, wait patiently, and watch for what He will do.

What circumstances spur you to try to bargain with God? How can it be both frightening and freeing to let go and surrender to His plan?

RECONCILED

RICK AND I HAVE known one another since fifth grade. We went out once during our freshman year of high school and then dated others while remaining good friends. When I was in my senior year of college and Rick was serving as a marine in Vietnam, we reconnected through correspondence. When he came home, I took one look and thought, *Wow, he sure grew up.* He thought the same about me. We fell in love fast and hard and married a year after he returned.

You'd think two people who were friends for so long would know each other well. But childhood friendship and a steamy courtship are far different than marriage. The realities of life together quickly surfaced. We both dragged baggage into our relationship. We experienced high highs and low lows. By the time we'd been married sixteen years and had three children, we were veterans of domestic warfare, both sides battle weary, with thoughts of divorce as a truce.

Where do you find a good mediator? Someone who loves you both and wants to help you put the pieces of your lives back together? We'd both stopped believing in "happily ever after."

Rescue is done *for* someone. Redemption also comes through the work of another—someone willing to pay the price for our mess so we can start fresh. Jesus rescued us from the captivity of our sins. He redeemed us before His Father through His death and resurrection. Reconciliation is different. It involves the cooperation of all parties involved. Reconciliation brings an end to estrangement and rebuilds a relationship. Jesus acted as a mediator and made the way for our reconciliation with Father God, and He can do the same thing in human relationships.

Rick and I both knew God had to be at the center of our marriage or we wouldn't make it to our seventeenth anniversary. How? When? We had no time for or with each other. We lived in a small rental house with three active school-age children. Rick had his own business and had to be in his office by 7:00 a.m. He worked six and a half days a week. When did we have time together? In bed. Sex may be a momentary "fix," but it's not a solution to serious relational problems.

How do you put God in the middle of a crumbling marriage, especially when you're both brand new to faith and still have doubts? Rick said we needed to spend time talking, and the only time we could be alone together to do that uninterrupted would be in the wee hours before he headed for work. That meant I had to get up much earlier than I normally did. I decided it was worth a try. Rick got up even earlier and fixed the coffee. We sat and read the Bible, talked, and prayed together. That time in the morning built our faith, rebuilt our individual lives, and blessed our marriage.

Two people can be reconciled when they enter a love triangle: with God at the top and the two individuals at the bottom points. As we each draw closer to God, we naturally draw closer to one another.

We still get up before dawn and have our time in the morning together. We recently celebrated our fiftieth wedding anniversary. True reconciliation is shown in changed lives and relationships.

Building Faith Through Prayer

THE CRUSH OF people made her more and more nervous. Where were they all going? What did they do for a living? Her head was throbbing. Maybe it was the hunger. Maybe it was worrying about what she was going to do when her gold ran out. Maybe it was knowing she was weak and would probably go right back to being a harlot just so she could keep body and soul together.

What am I going to do? God, I don't know what to do!

Go into that cafe and rest.

Angel looked up the street and saw a small cafe. Sighing, she walked toward it and went in. . . .

"Mister, you need a new cook," she said with a dry smile, setting the mug down and pushing the plate aside.

"You asking for employment? You're hired!"

Have you ever experienced God's direction in a tangible way?

Newly arrived in San Francisco with gold that would last only two or three more days, Angel had no idea where to go. Because of her love for Michael, she resolved not to go back to prostitution, but how else could she earn money? Worried and unsure, she prayed for help—and then heard God's voice.

Within minutes of entering the cafe where God had directed her, she had a job, a safe place to stay, and an employer who loved Jesus and would treat her well. It was more than she could have expected, and it had all fallen into her lap. God heard her prayer.

We don't always receive answers like this, of course. God works in all kinds of ways, and sometimes His answers are less clear. But God's answer in this case provided Angel with more than food and housing, as needed as those things were. His provision also showed her that He was listening, that He would speak to her, and that He cared.

Isn't that what answers to prayer do? I have several friends who received surprise gifts of money when they were in dire financial straits. Not only did those gifts cover their bills, but they grew my friends' belief that God would provide for them. When the next financial crisis hit, they trusted God more easily. They had already seen God at work, and they knew He could provide again.

I think that's one of the reasons Scripture instructs us to pray about things both big and small. Psalm 55:22 says, "Cast your burden upon the LORD and He will sustain you." Praying—giving our burden to God—and then seeing Him act is one of the ways our faith grows.

Throughout Scripture, the Israelites were instructed to remember their past history and how God acted on their behalf. This comes up often in the book of Deuteronomy, as the people left their life of slavery in Egypt and began a new life of freedom in the Promised Land. Moses instructed the people, "You shall remember that you were a slave in the land of Egypt, and the LORD your God brought you out of there by a mighty hand and by an outstretched arm" (Deuteronomy 5:15). Moses hoped that later, when the people were tempted to worship Canaanite idols, they would remember what God had done, which would remind them who they were: God's people, redeemed and set apart.

Sometimes the Israelites made altars of stone at locations where God acted mightily. In Joshua 3, God caused the waters of the Jordan River to collect in a heap upstream so that the people could cross safely. After everyone was on the other bank, Joshua gave instructions to the leaders of the twelve tribes:

> Cross again to the ark of the LORD your God into the middle of the Jordan, and each of you take up a stone on his shoulder, according to the number of the tribes of the sons of Israel. Let this be a sign among you, so that when your children ask later, saying, "What do these stones mean to you?" then you shall say to them, "Because the waters of the Jordan were cut off before the ark of the covenant of the LORD; when it crossed the Jordan, the waters of the Jordan were cut off." So these stones shall become a memorial to the sons of Israel forever. (Joshua 4:5–7)

For generations to come, anyone who passed by the altar would be reminded of what God had done.

What are the altars in our lives? They might be moments when we felt God's care and saw His specific answer to prayer, or they might be Scripture verses that anchor us to what God has done in the past. These are the things we must return to when we're afraid or when we doubt God is actually present in our lives.

God was calling Angel to Himself, preparing her for the moment when she would be ready to be fully reconciled to Him. By answering her prayer for guidance in this manner, He showed her she could trust Him more fully, even in the difficult challenges about to come.

If you are discouraged or wondering whether God cares, pray—about things both big and small. Watch for His answers, and let them build your faith. And while you're waiting, keep your mind focused on His promises. He has acted on your behalf before, and He will again. Cast your burdens on Him, for He cares for you.

Think back on your life, and try to identify a few occasions when you saw God answer prayer. How did those answered prayers affect your faith? Write these down, and look back at them when you begin to doubt His love and leading.

The Fruit of Suffering

MICHAEL SLOWED HIS *frenetic work and sought solace in God's word.* I don't understand anything anymore, Lord. Losing her is like losing half of myself. She loved me. I know she did. Why did you drive her from me?

The answer came to him slowly, with the changing of the seasons.

You shall have no other gods before me.

That couldn't be right.

Michael's anger grew. "When have I worshiped anyone but you?" *He raged again.* "I've followed you all my life. I've never put anyone before you." *Hands fisted, he wept.* "I love her, but I never made her my god."

In the calm that followed his angry torrent of words, Michael heard—and finally understood.

You became hers.

D o we trust that God has a reason for what He allows in our lives?

Michael hated what God was doing. He raged and grieved, filled with doubt and pain. Why had God taken Angel away? Why now, when at last she genuinely loved Michael and they were making a life together? Why rip them apart after He had brought them together? It didn't make sense.

Yet eventually, as God revealed Himself, Michael began to see. Angel had come to love him, yes, but not in the way he loved her—as a good gift from an even better God. Instead, Michael had become everything to her. Living with him and loving him left her no space to meet God for herself and understand who He really was.

Michael still didn't know whether Angel would ever come back, and his pain remained. But now he knew that God was at work. There was a purpose behind what was happening.

James 1:2–4 offers one of the most startling bits of wisdom in the epistles:

> Consider it all joy, my brethren, when you encounter various trials, knowing that the testing of your faith produces endurance. And let endurance have its perfect result, so that you may be perfect and complete, lacking in nothing.

How can we "consider it all joy" when we face trouble? No one rejoices in difficulty, but we can learn to rejoice in what the difficulty will produce in us.

Hard times help us grow. We don't like this, but we know it's true. Desperate situations clarify what's important and push us to call on God. When we're in trouble or facing big challenges, we are most aware of how inadequate we are and how much we need Him.

When have you been closest to God over the years? If you're like me, it's been when you were struggling the most, whether with loss, grief, anxiety, a family crisis, or any of a myriad of problems. In our hardest times, Scripture often comes alive, every passage speaking vital truth. In church, we might feel as if the songs were chosen for us. Our hearts become tender to others who are suffering. We pray more often because we need so much help. We feel God sustaining us in our hardest moments, even in the midst of the pain.

When things go smoothly, it's easy to drift away from God. Yes, we still love Him and know that He loves us, but we may not burn with the same desperate need for Him.

The same pattern is evident in the Bible. David was anointed Israel's next king at a young age. He gained renown by killing the Philistine giant Goliath and became immensely popular with the people—incurring the jealousy of the current king, Saul. His life after that contained several periods of extreme trouble, and some of his most distinctive psalms were written in the midst of them.

In Psalm 31, he called out for help when Saul was chasing him:

In You, O Lord, I have taken refuge;
Let me never be ashamed;
In Your righteousness deliver me.

Incline Your ear to me, rescue me quickly;
Be to me a rock of strength,
A stronghold to save me. (verses 1–2)

In Psalm 20, he focused on trust during times of war:

Some boast in chariots and some in horses,
But we will boast in the name of the LORD, our God.
    (verse 7)

In Psalm 3, he despaired when his son Absalom tried to take over the kingdom:

You, O LORD, are a shield about me,
My glory, and the One who lifts my head. (verse 3)

In Psalm 51, he grieved and repented after committing a great sin:

Create in me a clean heart, O God,
And renew a steadfast spirit within me.
Do not cast me away from Your presence
And do not take Your Holy Spirit from me.
Restore to me the joy of Your salvation
And sustain me with a willing spirit. (verses 10–12)

Suffering is painful but can produce great fruit in us. We may know people who have been through exceptionally difficult experiences and who believe going through those challenges brought them to a better life in the end. I think that's a view few take these days. We tend to ask "Why?" rather than "How can this experience strengthen and prepare me for what lies ahead?" Asking "Why?" can leave us feeling stuck, because we may never receive an answer. Thinking about the struggle as a means of growth can change our perspective and free us to move forward.

If you're in the midst of trouble and wondering why God would allow difficulty in your life, take the opportunity to draw near to Him. Consider how He might be working to reconcile you to Himself. Remember that He is with you through it all and that you can develop endurance and faith as you turn to Him.

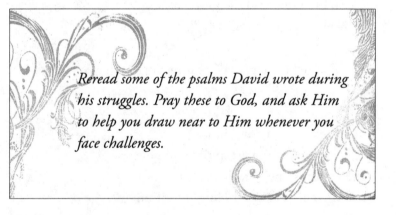

Reread some of the psalms David wrote during his struggles. Pray these to God, and ask Him to help you draw near to Him whenever you face challenges.

Prayers That Matter

MICHAEL AWAKENED IN a cold sweat. Angel had called to him. He had seen her standing in the midst of a fire, crying out his name over and over again. He couldn't get to her no matter how hard he tried, but he saw a dark figure walking through the flames toward her.

He ran shaking hands through his damp hair. Sweat was running down his bare chest, and he couldn't stop shaking. "It was just a dream."

The foreboding he felt was so heavy he was nauseated. He prayed. Then he rose from the bed and went outside. It would be dawn soon. Things would look better in the light of day. When dawn came, the sensation that something was wrong would not go away, and he prayed again, fervently. He was full of fear for his wife.

Where was she? How was she surviving? Was she hungry? Did she have shelter? How was she making her way alone?

Few things cause more anxiety than knowing that a friend or loved one is in trouble but not being able to help.

Michael was already dealing with the pain of not knowing where Angel was or what was happening to her. But when he dreamed about her in distress, calling for him, he experienced a heaviness and fear that wouldn't subside. Afraid to the point of being sick, he did the only thing he could: he prayed. All day he called out to God for the sake of his beloved wife.

Prayer is a mystery we'll never fully understand. We know God is sovereign and loving, so the idea of praying with the object of changing His mind or bringing issues to His attention might seem strange. At the same time, Scripture clearly encourages us to come to God with our burdens and requests. Prayer brings us into communion with God, helps us know Him better, and causes us to trust Him more as we see Him respond. Praying for others—taking the time to ask for God's help in their lives—is an act of love, reminding us that they are in His hands and that He loves them even more than we do. He knows and He cares.

Paul's epistles contain several beautiful prayers for believers in the churches he had founded. And *what* Paul prayed for them is illuminating:

> We have not stopped praying for you since we first heard about you. We ask God to give you complete knowledge of his will and to give you spiritual wisdom and understanding. Then the way you live will always honor and please the Lord, and your lives will produce

every kind of good fruit. All the while, you will grow as you learn to know God better and better.

We also pray that you will be strengthened with all his glorious power so you will have all the endurance and patience you need. (Colossians 1:9–11, NLT)

Our prayers for others are often focused on circumstances. We pray about illnesses, school and job issues, busy schedules, and money problems. These are all vitally important in our lives, and God cares about them. But too often we forget to pray about the bigger issues behind our circumstances.

Paul's first concern for the Colossians was their standing with God. He prayed they would grow to know Him better. He prayed for their wisdom and fruitfulness. He prayed God would strengthen them and give them the endurance they needed to face whatever the future held in a way that would honor Him.

That's a powerful prayer. And sometimes the answer to this kind of prayer looks far different than we expect.

If Michael had known what was happening to Angel, he would have done everything he could to get her away from Duke as quickly as possible—even fighting his way through a room full of men. Yet God chose to work a different way. He was allowing Angel to experience this darkness without Michael so she could begin to understand he was not her savior. She had been rescued from prostitution months earlier, but now God was setting the pieces in place to reconcile her fully to Himself. That was ultimately what Michael had been praying for Angel—but he never could have guessed the way God intended to answer.

When we're at the end of our rope or when we see a loved one in dire circumstances, praying for relief is always a good thing to do. But we can go deeper and pray for more. We can pray that our struggles will cause us to see God more clearly. To understand what is most important. To experience His love in a deeper way. To learn more about following Him.

We never have to pray perfectly. Romans 8:26–27 tells us that we have help from the Holy Spirit, who intercedes for us:

> In the same way the Spirit also helps our weakness; for we do not know how to pray as we should, but the Spirit Himself intercedes for us with groanings too deep for words; and He who searches the hearts knows what the mind of the Spirit is, because He intercedes for the saints according to the will of God.

If you're afraid for yourself or for others, ask God to work mightily in the circumstances—and to draw everyone involved closer to Him. We don't always know how God will answer our prayers. But we can trust that the Reconciler is always at work.

Write out Paul's prayer from Colossians 1, and put it somewhere you'll see it each day. Make a habit of praying it for yourself and those around you.

Seeing Jesus

HER NIGHTMARES RETURNED. . . .

She could hardly stand under the weight of the filth clinging to her. She staggered onto the beach and sank down, exhausted. Her skin was blotched with ugly sores and disgusting growths.

She looked up and saw Michael standing before her. A small flame burned where his heart was. **No, beloved.** *His mouth hadn't moved, and the voice was not his. The flame grew larger and brighter, spreading until his entire body was radiant with it. Then the light separated from Michael and came the last few feet toward her. It was a man, glorious and magnificent, light streaming from him in all directions.*

"Who are you?" she whispered, terrified. "Who are you?"

Yahweh, El Shaddai, Jehovah-mekoddishkem, El Elyon, El Olam, Elohim . . .

The names kept coming, moving together like music, rushing through her blood, filling her. She trembled in fear and could not move. He reached out and touched her, and she felt warmth encompassing her and the fear dissolving away. She looked down at herself and found she was clean and clothed in white.

Everything changes when we see Jesus for who He really is. Angel had built up years of bitterness against God. The terrible circumstances she had endured, the lack of compassion and forgiveness she and her mother had experienced from the church, and her own parents' and grandparents' failures all combined to convince her that God was no one she wanted to know. She assumed He would reject her anyway, so what was the point? She told Michael that God had never been there for her. She was convinced He didn't care at all.

Yet through Michael's example of faith, she saw that God might be different than she had imagined and that Michael's fierce love, forgiveness, and compassion might be an echo of God Himself. But even with this realization, she was still stunned when she saw an image of Jesus in her dream—not as a beaten-down man but as He is now. Glorified. Powerful. Radiant.

In the book of Revelation, the apostle John recorded his own reaction to seeing the glorified Jesus:

> In the middle of the lampstands I saw one like a son of man, clothed in a robe reaching to the feet, and girded across His chest with a golden sash. His head and His hair were white like white wool, like snow; and His eyes were like a flame of fire. His feet were like burnished

bronze, when it has been made to glow in a furnace, and
His voice was like the sound of many waters. In His
right hand He held seven stars, and out of His mouth
came a sharp two-edged sword; and His face was like the
sun shining in its strength.

When I saw Him, I fell at His feet like a dead man.
And He placed His right hand on me, saying, "Do not
be afraid; I am the first and the last, and the living One;
and I was dead, and behold, I am alive forevermore, and
I have the keys of death and of Hades." (1:13–18)

John had spent years with Jesus during His time on earth.
They had eaten together and traveled together. They knew
each other very well—yet even so, John was awed at the sight
of the resurrected and glorified Jesus.

And who wouldn't be? This image of Jesus is far beyond
the illustrations we see in children's storybooks. Eyes like a
flame of fire, feet like burnished bronze, a sword in His
mouth, His face like the sun. The details may not matter as
much as the overall impression: Power. Authority. Beauty.
Glory. This image would be terrifying if it weren't for Jesus's
words to John, starting with "Do not be afraid." Jesus reminds
John who He is.

Later in Revelation, Jesus spoke these words: "Let the one
who is thirsty come; let the one who wishes take the water of
life without cost" (22:17). Jesus—the Alpha and Omega, the
powerful One, the One who was dead and now is alive
forevermore—invites us to come to Him. He offers "the water
of life" without any cost to us! He calls us to Himself to be
forgiven and to be reconciled to Him.

Angel's dream laid everything out clearly. She knew she was sinful—the imagined filth covering her revealed that. She was helpless on her own. She thought it was Michael coming to save her, but he wouldn't be able to help her without becoming filthy himself. Only Jesus could call her and cleanse her—and still remain spotless.

Jesus's words to her are His words to us: *I am the way. Follow Me.* He calls us each by name because He knows us. He calls us to follow because He wants us to be saved. He wants us to find the way to Him, to eternal life, and to love and forgiveness.

We know the Jesus of the Gospels—the One who taught and healed. But let us never forget that what the disciples saw on earth is not the entirety of who Jesus is. He died and was raised. He is glorified in heaven, sitting at the right hand of God. He is full of power and authority and majesty—and also love and compassion and forgiveness. He calls us to be reconciled to Him.

If your faith is stagnant and you're not sure where to go from here, look at the person of Jesus. Remember who He is and what He calls us to.

Spend some time meditating on the Revelation passage, and imagine what John saw. How does it change your perception of Jesus to imagine Him the way John described Him?

God's Power in Weakness

OH, GOD. OH, Jesus, please help me!

"He's almost got them ready for you."

Then, just when she thought her heart would stop for the terror, she heard it.

Sarah, beloved.

It was the same soft voice she had heard in Michael's cabin. The one she'd heard in her dream . . .

Be still, for I am here.

Angel closed her eyes tightly again, trying to block out the maddening crowd sitting in front of the stage, trying to focus on the frightening, quiet voice in her head that called her by a name she had heard only once in a dream since her mother died.

She opened her eyes, and suddenly the shaking inside her stopped. She couldn't explain it, but she felt calm. Unnaturally so. She stepped forward, and the guard held the curtain aside so she could walk out.

❧

When it seems that there is no escape, God provides a way—and displays His power for all to see.

Angel stood backstage, listening to the catcalls of the men waiting to ogle her. She panicked, seeing no way out of the hell Duke planned for her. But in the midst of the noise and commotion, at a moment when she felt most powerless and hopeless, a still, small voice called her by name. ***Sarah, beloved.***

In this horrible place, on the brink of what looked as if it would rank among the worst experiences of an already difficult life, this young woman, who had long felt abandoned and condemned by God, heard Him call her. She still wasn't sure what was going to happen, but she knew He was present. The God she hardly believed in knew her by name. He loved her. In that moment when she had to walk onstage, that was enough. Even in the uncertainty, she had been given a calm she couldn't explain.

Isaiah 43 begins with a powerful statement about God's presence in the hardest circumstances:

Thus says the LORD, your Creator, O Jacob,
And He who formed you, O Israel,
"Do not fear, for I have redeemed you;
I have called you by name; you are Mine!
"When you pass through the waters, I will be with you;
And through the rivers, they will not overflow you.
When you walk through the fire, you will not be
    scorched,

Nor will the flame burn you.

"For I am the LORD your God,

The Holy One of Israel, your Savior." (verses 1–3)

In this life, we will face struggles, many of them desperate. We will have to pass through waters and walk through the fire, but God will be with us. Though at times we feel surrounded by evil, He will not let us be overcome by it. No matter what happens, no matter what hardships we face, His love surrounds us. His presence never leaves us.

What a gift. It transforms every situation we will ever encounter, every battle we have to fight.

Perhaps we, like Angel, have spent years trying to win battles on our own. We might fight our circumstances with anger, defensiveness, sarcasm, or withdrawal. Or we might arm ourselves with logic or intellect. We've learned to depend on ourselves and utilize all the tools at our disposal. But God calls us to lay down those weapons and pick up His instead. Because when we do—when we trust not in our own natural skills or tendencies but in Him—we allow His power to work through us. And unexpected things happen.

Angel's natural tendency was to protect herself by withdrawing emotionally, putting on a hard shell of disdain. But when she went onstage, God prompted her to look into the eyes of the men in the casino. When she did, she saw despair, not just vice, and a deeper need, not just lust. She felt compassion for the men—and that changed the whole situation.

In 2 Corinthians 12:7, Paul wrote about his own "thorn in the flesh" that he kept asking God to take away. God said no, telling him, "My grace is all you need. My power works best in weakness." Paul's response is remarkable: "Now I am glad to boast about my weaknesses, so that the power of Christ can work through me" (verse 9, NLT).

What does it look like to boast about our weaknesses? Perhaps it means we no longer try to put on a brave front, like a puffer fish inflating itself to several times its normal size to protect itself from predators. Instead of covering up our weak spots, we allow others to see them, showing that we depend on God for everything we accomplish. We aren't doing anything in our own strength. We are weak, but He is strong. He chooses to work through us.

When we get out of the way, setting aside our natural inclinations and responses, God's presence can be seen more clearly. Others can tell that God's power is at work. And we can rejoice in the amazing knowledge that we have been a part of the reconciling work God is doing in the world.

If you feel weak and unable to handle things on your own, let it be an opportunity to depend on God. Pray that His work will be seen clearly in you.

Think about how you usually respond to difficulties. How would things change if you stopped defending yourself and instead let your weaknesses show, depending on God's power to work through you?

DAY 34

The Fragrance of Christ

SHE LOOKED AROUND at the men again, all silent now, stunned. Some couldn't meet her eyes but looked away, ashamed.

"Why are you all here?" she cried out, the tears so close she was afraid they would choke her. "Why aren't you home with your wives and children, or your mothers and sisters? Don't you know what this place is? Don't you know where you are?"

Angel walked slowly off the stage. She saw Duke waiting for her, a look in his eyes that she had never seen before. Perspiration beaded his brow, and his face was pale with fury. He grabbed her arm brutally and yanked her into the shadows. "What made you do a stupid thing like that?"

"God, I think," she said, stunned. She felt jubilation—and the presence of a power so immense she was trembling. She looked up at Duke and wasn't afraid of him anymore.

"God?" He spat the word out. His eyes blazed. "I'm going to kill you. I should have killed you a long time ago."

*"You're afraid, aren't you? I can smell it. You're afraid of
something you can't even see. And do you know why? Because
what Michael has is more powerful than you ever were, ever
could be."*

⸎

How do people respond when they see Christ in us?
Angel wasn't sure what she was supposed to do onstage, but in the calmness she knew had come from God, she
did what seemed best. She sang the song God brought to
mind—"Rock of Ages." She spoke truth to the men, reminding them of their families and making them consider why
they were choosing this poor substitute for life-giving relationships. As she did, others saw God working through her.

Some of the men perceived it and were ashamed. Shocked
to hear a hymn in a casino, they were convicted of their own
sin and weakness and glimpsed God's love and power. Perhaps
some of them took a step toward repentance and reconciliation with God. Others hardened their hearts, turning away
from deeper introspection. These men cheered and clapped as
soon as the bawdy entertainment resumed. Still others, like
Duke, saw and were afraid.

Duke's entire life had been built around his sense of power.
He took the girls he wanted and abused them. He held others
captive and hopeless. He hurt anyone who stood in his way.
He staked his life on the fact that nothing existed beyond the
material world and that no one could hold him accountable.
So he was terrified by the idea that Someone existed whom he
couldn't see or control—Someone more powerful than he.

The apostle Paul wrote about this reaction in 2 Corinthians 2:

> [God] uses us to spread the knowledge of Christ every-
> where, like a sweet perfume. Our lives are a Christ-like
> fragrance rising up to God. But this fragrance is per-
> ceived differently by those who are being saved and by
> those who are perishing. To those who are perishing, we
> are a dreadful smell of death and doom. But to those
> who are being saved, we are a life-giving perfume.
> (verses 14–16, NLT)

Why are we "a dreadful smell of death and doom" to those
who have rejected God? Because we are a reminder that they
are not in control of their own lives and destinies. No matter
how powerful they are, God is stronger. They may have established their own set of rules for life—rules that tilt everything
to their advantage—but God reveals through us that they do
not write the real rules. To those who think they are in control
and have no intention of changing, the truth of Christ is
frightening. But to those who know they need Him, who are
being drawn to Him, it is life giving. The fragrance is like
sweet perfume.

When Angel spoke those words of truth, she wasn't re-
sponsible for the outcome. That was between the individual
men and God. Her role—and ours—is to allow others to see
the powerful presence of God in our lives. The apostle Paul
wrote, "I am not ashamed of this Good News about Christ. It
is the power of God at work, saving everyone who believes"
(Romans 1:16, NLT).

Angel was full of jubilation when she came offstage, not

because she had accomplished something great, but because God had used her to accomplish more than she could even have imagined. He wasn't just saving her by getting her away from Duke. He was showing her who He was. He was saving Cherry and Faith and others. He was calling some of the men to repentance. And He was revealing the truth about Duke so that he would no longer be able to hurt these women. All from a half-remembered song and a few words. All in one moment of God's power on display.

Psalm 77 reminds us of God's mighty power at work for our redemption:

> Your way, O God, is holy;
> What god is great like our God?
> You are the God who works wonders;
> You have made known Your strength among the peoples.
> You have by Your power redeemed Your people. (verses
>   13–15)

If you question how our God can use you, remember you are spreading the fragrance of Christ wherever you go. His presence in you is powerful.

How can you spread more of the fragrance of Christ? Ask God to guide you when you are in situations where you can show His truth to others.

Come to Me

ANGEL DRANK IN the words of salvation and redemption though she felt she had no right to them. She was so hungry and thirsty, she panted like a deer after the water of life— remembering as she listened the dream she had had in Duke's bordello in Portsmouth Square.

Oh, God, it was you speaking to me, wasn't it? It was you. And that night in the cabin so long ago when I smelled that wonderful fragrance and thought I heard someone speaking to me, it was you.

Everything Michael had said to her, everything he had done, made sense to her now. He had lived Christ so that she could understand.

Oh, Lord, why was I so blind. Why couldn't I hear? Why did it take so much pain for me to see that you have been there reaching out to me all along?

The still, quiet voice beckoned tenderly.

Come to me, beloved. Stand and come to me.

Warmth swept over her. This was the love she'd been waiting for all her life.

C*ome to me.*

God had been speaking to Angel all along, but she hadn't been able to hear it over her pain and bitterness. Slowly He had broken down her defenses—through Michael's steadfast love, through the example of Miriam and the Altmans, through the kindness of the Axles, and through the powerful words of Scripture. Most of all, His still, small voice had called to her in her dream and at her worst moment in Duke's casino. His power had delivered her when she still wasn't sure she believed. Now she was finally able to hear Him. **Come to me.**

He offered everything she needed. She had been thirsting for His love for years, throughout all her struggles and anger and suffering, but she hadn't realized it. His love was perfect and full of forgiveness. His love wanted what was best for her and gave new meaning to her life. Michael's love had been wonderful and had set her on this path, but his love alone wasn't enough.

Jesus told His followers, "I am the bread of life; he who comes to Me will not hunger, and he who believes in Me will never thirst" (John 6:35). Longings fill our hearts and minds, but our desires can't be quenched by anything in this world. Only God's love can fully satisfy.

Jeremiah 31:3 says, "I have loved you, my people, with an everlasting love. With unfailing love I have drawn you to myself" (NLT). His love won't let us go. If we listen, we can hear the still, small voice calling us to come to Him.

Too often we ignore it. We busy ourselves with the seemingly urgent things on our to-do lists. We distract ourselves with mindless entertainment. We drown out His voice with other voices—others' expectations, our fears and anxieties, the world's call to success. Some days we ignore our desperate thirst and go about our lives as if God isn't really there.

Angel heard God calling her to accept His forgiveness and become His child. That's the first and most important invitation anyone can receive. Accepting it brings us from death to life, from darkness to light. We gain forgiveness, the promise of eternal life, and true communion with God.

But those of us who answered that call long ago sometimes forget that, while our salvation was settled once and for all, part of responding to God's love means abiding in Him every moment of every day. It means allowing Him to satisfy our need for love and safety and letting Him fill our lives with meaning.

Come to me.

When we learn to recognize the still, small voice of God, we hear it calling us to draw near and be reconciled to Him. To stop fighting and surrender. To relinquish our pride, to set aside the things we've been using to distract us, and to walk with obedience into His unfailing love.

The apostle Paul showed us what reconciliation with God looks like:

> You were his enemies, separated from him by your evil
> thoughts and actions. Yet now he has reconciled you to

himself through the death of Christ in his physical body.
As a result, he has brought you into his own presence,
and you are holy and blameless as you stand before him
without a single fault.

But you must continue to believe this truth and
stand firmly in it. Don't drift away from the assurance
you received when you heard the Good News. (Colossians 1:21–23, NLT)

If you feel that you are drifting away, don't let another day
go by without drawing close to Him. Let Angel's story remind
you of the beauty and transforming power of God's love. Reread Scripture to remind you. Come close to God through
prayer. Talk with other believers about Him. Stand firm in the
assurance that He, in His deep love, has reconciled you to
Himself.

This is the love we've been waiting for all our lives. Let's
seize the gift.

*How is God calling you? Where might He
be asking you to go deeper, get closer, and live
more fully in faith?*

RESTORED

Is RESTORATION A REBOOT? A chance to go back and begin afresh? To reinstate what was meant to be before Adam took the fruit from Eve's hand and chose to eat it and divorce God?

Being restored brought far-reaching changes in my life. Through Christ's work on the cross, I am restored to the relationship with God that He created me to have: I am now His child, His friend, one who enjoys a close, intimate relationship with Him. I can freely talk with Him anywhere, anytime, and He hears and loves me. Whatever happens, God brings good purpose from and through it because I love Him and I am His. And this restored relationship, meant from the beginning of creation, is not temporal but eternal.

I *decided* to accept Jesus as my Savior and Lord. It wasn't an emotional high, a blinding-light-born-again experience that some have. I can't even tell you the day it happened. I can only tell you I knew without a doubt that I was a sinner, that my choices were the cause of my misery, and that I'd done everything I knew how to do on my own to find peace, contentment, purpose, fulfillment—and failed. My decision to believe Jesus meant complete, not half-hearted, surrender. The turning point happened in silence and with a simple prayer: *Okay, God. I give up. I've made a complete mess of my life. You can have it. Do whatever You want.* And His answer was restoration.

Did I have immediate relief? No. Did I suddenly have all the answers I wanted? No, but I had access to the One who does. Did things change? Yes, but not as quickly as I hoped, although some prayers were answered right away, such as having a desire to read and study the Bible. From His Word I learned God wasn't who the world said He was. I felt no condemnation, found no list of good deeds to do in order to feel His love, and discovered no deadline. My vision of life did change. The Light of the world poured in and opened my eyes and ears to absorb things in a new way.

Remember how I thought my mother rejected me? When I looked at my childhood from this new perspective, I understood her actions differently. She had been diagnosed with tuberculosis when I was young and had to be quarantined in her bedroom. My brother and I were tested every few months. When my mother said, "Get out of my room," she was really saying, "I love you too much to expose you to a disease that can kill you." Now I realized she had shown me sacrificial love.

Each time I read the Bible, the Lord met me where I was, spoke to me in a way I could understand, and showed me where and how to realign my life with His. (That's still true.) I was a writer, but then I suddenly couldn't write . . . until I felt God telling me to use the gift He had given me to draw closer to Him. So, I did, and I waited in expectation of those amazing aha moments of epiphany. My writing became an open window to my personal struggles and how God loves us and is ever present. He gives each believer the Holy Spirit to teach and guide us through life.

I had once thought I was rejected, but I found myself loved. I had felt resigned, but I learned God offers abundant life for those who trust in Him. I had been held captive in sin but was rescued by Jesus through the cross. I was lost, but He redeemed me from death and hell. When I accepted Jesus as my Savior and Lord, I became reconciled to God and restored to the intimate relationship my soul longed to have.

Still, there are times when I feel the tension of living in the lifelong process of transformation, of living between now and Jesus's finished work. This temporal life is a struggle. I am a new creation, but I'm still far from Christlike. He dwells in me, but I still struggle with my fleshly nature. I am not the woman I want to be, yet I'm far from the woman I was.

This I know: God's love is constant. He is faithful to complete the work in me. I imagine myself sometimes in my Father's lap, my head resting against His heart, His arms around me. No matter what comes, I am safe in Him. In every battle in which I get entangled, I remind myself: Jesus already won the war. The Holy Spirit within me is a seal of promise and also the consuming fire of God, cleansing and refining me for complete restoration, for when I meet God face to face.

DAY 36

Making Sense of the Past

JONATHAN NOTICED THE difference in Angel immediately. Her face was aglow, and the smile she wore was one of joy. "I know what God wants me to do with my life," she said, sitting on the edge of the sofa.

She told them about meeting Torie and lunching with her. She told them of the young prostitute's dejection and hopelessness and how she had felt the same way for so many years.

"Torie said if she could find a way out, she'd take it. Virgil asked if she could cook, and she said no. And it came to me, right there in Virgil's. Why not?"

"Why not what?" Susanna said, exasperated. "You're making no sense."

"Why not give her a way out," Angel said. "Teach her to cook. Teach her to sew. Teach her to make hats. Teach her anything that would give her another way to make a living. Jona-

than, I want to buy a house where someone like Torie can come and be safe and learn to earn her own living without selling her body to do it."

✦

Have you ever had a moment where your past pain suddenly made sense?

Angel had come to faith in God and was living in that new reality, knowing Him more and more. That brought her joy, as did living with the Axles—yet she lived in limbo, knowing there was something else she should be doing with her life. She had prayed for God's direction and waited for His response. Then, suddenly, it all made sense.

Who knew better than Angel what it was like for a woman to be stuck in a life she hated? Who knew better how years of bitterness and degradation could isolate a woman and fill her heart with despair? And who knew better how hope could be restored and how God could transform a heart and life? Angel was the perfect person to reach out to women who needed rescue, meaningful work, faith, and hope.

Everything she had experienced, from the worst moments to the best, had prepared her for this moment, this mission. God was redeeming everything that had been meant for evil and was using it for her good and His glory. It seemed impossible—but nothing is impossible with God.

Romans 8:28 is a wonderful but hard verse: "We know that God causes everything to work together for the good of those who love God and are called according to his purpose for them" (NLT). It's even harder when we think about a story like Angel's. *Everything?* All the abuse she had experienced at the hands of others—how can that be used for good?

Only God can make that happen.

The classic scriptural example is Joseph, whose jealous brothers sold him into slavery and then told his father he was dead. He ended up in Egypt, jailed because of false allegations. While there, he interpreted dreams for two other prisoners. Later, when Pharaoh was having troubling dreams of his own, one of them recommended he consult Joseph. Joseph correctly interpreted the dreams and was appointed Pharaoh's second-in-command, and God used Joseph to save Egypt and the surrounding lands from famine. Years later, when his brothers came to Egypt to buy food and discovered who he was, he told them, "You intended to harm me, but God intended it all for good. He brought me to this position so I could save the lives of many people" (Genesis 50:20, NLT).

It might be easy to look at someone else's life—especially someone in the Bible—and see how God used bad things for good. But it's far more difficult to see it in our own lives when we're walking through hardships, isn't it? It would be easier if we knew exactly what was going to result from our struggles, if we could see the happy ending in the midst of the pain. It's another thing to live blind, not knowing how God will turn around whatever right now seems hopeless. But our God is one who restores—not only us but also our circumstances and the world.

God's purposes are bigger than we can see or understand.

We look at this day, this week, and this year, but God looks at the scope of eternity. Our problems fill our field of vision, but God's view is broader. He is less concerned with what is easiest for us and more concerned with what is best. And His ultimate best for us involves our being restored to Him.

Look at the verses that follow Romans 8:28:

> God knew his people in advance, and he chose them to become like his Son, so that his Son would be the first-born among many brothers and sisters. And having chosen them, he called them to come to him. And having called them, he gave them right standing with himself. And having given them right standing, he gave them his glory. (verses 29–30, NLT)

God works in our lives to bring us to a right standing with Him. His goal is our ultimate good—our salvation—and His glory. And He can use *everything* to bring us closer to that goal. No matter how hurtful or senseless a situation seems now, He can make it new.

One day we will see how God has redeemed the world, taking away all sorrow and pain and death. None of those hard things will last. What will last is God Himself dwelling among us, those whom He has made His children. He will restore everything. Nothing will be wasted.

Write down a few of the hardest things in your life. Pray and hand them over to God, telling Him that while you don't know how He can possibly redeem these or use them for good, you will trust that He will. Make a note to reassess these hard things in a few months to see what God has been doing.

Freedom in Forgiveness

ANGEL'S MOUTH TREMBLED. "Paul, I'm so sorry for the pain I've caused you. Truly, I am."

He sat for a long time, unable to speak, thinking of all the time and all the persecution she had endured. From him. And now she *was* apologizing. He had plotted her destruction and destroyed himself in the process. From that time, he had been consumed by hatred, blinded by it. I have been insufferable and self-righteous and cruel. The revelation was bitter and painful, but a relief, too. There was an odd sort of freedom in standing before a mirror and seeing himself clearly. For the first time in his life.

Remorse overwhelmed him. It hurt to look at her. It hurt even more to see the truth—that he was greatly to blame for Michael's pain as well. If he had reached out just once as Miriam had said, maybe things would have been different, but he had been too proud, too sure he was right.

"I'm *sorry,*" he said. "So very sorry. Can you forgive me?"

Sometimes our blinders come off, and we can instantly see clearly.

Paul had harbored his hatred for Angel for years, ever since he had given her a ride to Pair-a-Dice and then demanded the only form of payment she had. She threw his betrayal of Michael in his face, and he had spent the next years trying to cover up his guilt by pretending she held all the blame. Letting go of his hatred would have meant admitting his own wrongdoing, so he held on tight, taking every opportunity to hurt Angel with his words and looks. But his hate had cost him almost more than it had cost her, keeping him bitter and resentful even years after she had left home.

And now, in just a few minutes of conversation, the scales had fallen off his eyes. Angel had left, not because she didn't love Michael, but because she did. She had given up love and safety and security because she thought it was best for Michael. And now Paul was face to face with his own sin and ugliness and guilt. He couldn't avoid them any longer.

What shocked him after all this time was the sense of relief that came from seeing himself clearly, from admitting what he had done. Being honest about his own failure freed him.

In Psalm 32, David presented a vivid picture of how it looks to try to hide our sin from God:

> When I refused to confess my sin,
>   my body wasted away,
>   and I groaned all day long.

Day and night your hand of discipline was heavy on me.
My strength evaporated like water in the summer
heat.

Finally, I confessed all my sins to you
and stopped trying to hide my guilt.
I said to myself, "I will confess my rebellion to the
LORD."
And you forgave me! All my guilt is gone. (verses
3–5, NLT)

When we try to cover up our sin, it's because we've forgotten the freedom that comes from admitting the truth. We're so used to hiding that we forget what it feels like to be fully known and forgiven. But when we confess, we're acknowledging to ourselves and God what stands between us. We're admitting we need forgiveness. Only then can we receive it—and be restored.

Forgiveness is also the path to restoring our relationships with others. Paul felt a huge weight lift when he confessed to Angel all the ways he had hurt her and asked for her forgiveness. After all this time and pain, the rift in their relationship could mend.

In Colossians, the apostle Paul wrote about the way believers should treat each other:

As those who have been chosen of God, holy and beloved, put on a heart of compassion, kindness, humility, gentleness and patience; bearing with one another, and forgiving each other, whoever has a complaint against anyone; just as the Lord forgave you, so also should you. Beyond all these things put on love, which is the perfect bond of unity. (3:12–14)

Love and forgiveness help set believers apart. They're a witness to the world because they are not a natural reaction. After a gunman burst into an Amish one-room schoolhouse in Pennsylvania and killed five girls, the world was stunned by the community's response. Even while grieving, they made a point to forgive the killer. Some attended his burial service and hugged his widow. They donated money to his family and brought them food.* The Amish community's ability to set aside a desire for revenge was a testimony not to their inherent goodness but to God's forgiveness working through them.

Forgiving others means letting go of hurts we hold on to and releasing our need to have the last word. The reward is a restored relationship, where past wrongs no longer stand in the way of love and fellowship. We can meet each other's eyes again and not need to tiptoe around what happened before. When wrongs have been openly acknowledged and let go, we can move forward.

Paul and Angel's every interaction had once been full of tension and conflict. Now each of them would be a reminder to the other of God's goodness rather than a reminder of his or her own failure. Their relationship would be a testimony of God's restoration.

---

* Joseph Shapiro, "Amish Forgive School Shooter, Struggle with Grief," NPR, October 2, 2007, www.npr.org/templates/story/story.php?storyId=14900930.

Are you in a hard relationship? How might it be transformed and restored by the power of forgiveness? Remember that God's forgiveness enables us to forgive others.

Is there someone you need to forgive or seek forgiveness from? Ask for God's help and resolve to make a phone call, write a letter, or meet with that person as you aim to restore your relationship.

A Bridge to Christ

SOMETIMES SHE TRIED *not to think about Michael at all because the pain was so great. But the hunger for him was always there, the endless, aching hunger. Only he had opened himself to be used in her life by Christ. Through him, Christ had been able to fill her until she was overflowing. Michael had always said it was God; now she knew that was true.*

And the knowledge that he'd been the bridge between her and her Savior only made her long for Michael all the more.

How can I not say thank you to him? Did I ever really explain what he did for me? What have I ever given him back but grief? *But she had gifts to offer him now. She had stood firm against Duke. She had walked the road Michael had taught her. Because of it, people had trusted her and backed her in building the House of Magdalena. She was doing good with her life, and it was all because of him, because of what she*

*had seen in him. "Seek and ye shall find," he'd read to her, and
she had.*

Who has helped you on your journey of faith? Who has
shown you Christ through his or her words and actions?

After Paul's visit, Angel reflected on all that Michael had
given her. It was only through him that she had arrived at the
life and faith she had now. He had rescued her from a life of
degradation and had nursed her back to health after her beating from Magowan—but that was just the beginning. He had
loved her through betrayal and hostility and days when he
was sure she would never return his love. He had given to her
generously, withholding nothing. He read Scripture to her
and explained it when she didn't understand. He responded
patiently to her anger and encouraged her when she felt insecure. He prayed for her. He had let her in to his life and shown
her what it looked like to follow God.

He showed her the good news of Christ, even when she
wasn't ready to see it, even when she rejected it. His life laid
the groundwork that allowed her to later respond to God's
call. Michael had been her bridge to faith.

None of us come to faith alone. No matter our backgrounds, we all have people in our lives who helped point us
to the truth. A pastor who faithfully explained Scripture. A
grandparent who prayed for us regularly. A friend who stood
by us during a hard time and showed us there was still hope.

A teacher who encouraged us. A coworker who invited us to a Bible study. A parent who modeled what it meant to put faith into practice. These people are gifts that God has placed in our paths. And maybe we have been fortunate enough to be that kind of gift to someone else.

The apostle John, in one of his epistles, wrote, "I have no greater joy than this, to hear of my children walking in the truth" (3 John 1:4). Can we relate? Our lives should have a lasting impact, and what better way than to help another person find God or know Him better. What joy to be able to look back on our lives and see that God used something we did or said to help another take a step toward Him.

In the Sermon on the Mount, Jesus told His listeners how they should live to have an impact on others:

> You are the light of the world. A city set on a hill cannot be hidden; nor does anyone light a lamp and put it under a basket, but on the lampstand, and it gives light to all who are in the house. Let your light shine before men in such a way that they may see your good works, and glorify your Father who is in heaven. (Matthew 5:14–16)

How do we let our light shine? Of course we'll never be perfect, but we reflect the One who is. We want others to see that we live differently because we love Him and know that He loves us. We want others to see us striving to do what is right—not because we're seeking to gain His favor but because we already have received it. We want others to see that we live in dependence on a perfect God, the source of all light, who restores us and can restore them.

If you wonder how you can have an impact on the world, think about how you might show God's love to those around you today. It doesn't need to be something big. Pray with someone. Send a note, bring food, or take a moment to talk to people around you who are having a hard time. Share an encouraging scripture. Point them to Christ. Let your light shine.

Take some time to think about people who have been influential in your life and have helped you develop your faith in God. Write a letter or email to one or two of them, letting them know how you're doing now and how their words or actions have influenced you.

DAY 39

God's Transforming Love

WEEPING, ANGEL SANK to her knees. Hot tears fell on his boots. She wiped them away with her hair. She bent over, heartbroken, and put her hands on his feet. "Oh, Michael, Michael, I'm sorry . . ."

Oh, God, forgive me.

She felt his hand on her head. "My love," he said. He took hold of her and drew her up again. She couldn't look into his face, wanting to hide her own. Michael took off his shirt and put it around her shoulders. When he tipped her chin up, she had no choice but to look into his eyes again. They were wet like hers but filled with light. "I hoped you would come home someday," he said and smiled.

"There's so much I have to say. So many things to tell you."

He combed his fingers into her flowing hair and tilted her head back. "We have the rest of our lives."

She thought she had been saved by his love for her, and in part she had been. It had cleansed her, never casting blame. But that had been only the beginning. It was loving him in return that had brought her up out of the darkness.

L ove transforms.

We see over and over again through the story of *Redeeming Love* that Angel was transformed by Michael's love. Through him, she experienced selfless love for the first time. Through him, she began to trust that there was good in the world and that God might be more concerned with forgiveness than with condemnation. Michael's love removed her insecurity and helped her open herself to hope and faith. It transformed her. Yet his love for her wasn't the sole source of her change. Being loved was the first step. Loving back was the next.

Loving Michael brought Angel hope that she was not ruined and still had the capacity to care about someone else. Earlier, her primary goal had been solitude—a life by herself in her own cabin—but now she found joy in having her life entwined with others and even being needed. She thought about Michael's well-being more than her own, and that led to sacrificing her own happiness. The very fact that she could do something not in her own self-interest indicated that something beyond her was at work. She sensed the possibility that God was real.

Loving others changes us. Whether we are parenting a child, caring for a loved one, living with a spouse, or supporting a friend or family member during a hard time, sometimes we look back at the way we used to be and can hardly recognize ourselves. We've learned—often through tough circumstances and always imperfectly—how to put others first. And when we love that way, we're mirroring God.

The apostle John wrote about the power of God's love:

> Dear friends, let us continue to love one another, for love comes from God. Anyone who loves is a child of God and knows God. But anyone who does not love does not know God, for God is love.
>
> God showed how much he loved us by sending his one and only Son into the world so that we might have eternal life through him. This is real love—not that we loved God, but that he loved us and sent his Son as a sacrifice to take away our sins.
>
> Dear friends, since God loved us that much, we surely ought to love each other. No one has ever seen God. But if we love each other, God lives in us, and his love is brought to full expression in us. (1 John 4:7–12, NLT)

Reread that last verse: "If we love each other, God lives in us, and his love is brought to full expression in us." When we love others sacrificially, we love—at least in some small human way—like God. That transforms not only us but those our love touches.

Michael's selfless love changed Angel. Angel's selfless love changed Paul, once he saw it for what it was, and it changed the young women Angel worked with at the House of Magdalena. Those who see selfless love will be drawn to it and transformed by it.

In John 13, Jesus spoke to His disciples during the Last Supper. He told them, "A new commandment I give to you, that you love one another, even as I have loved you, that you also love one another. By this all men will know that you are My disciples, if you have love for one another" (verse 34–35). Our love for others, as imperfect as it is, points to the only perfect love, offered by God to all, which is capable of restoring us and making us more like Him.

How has loving others changed you? Thank God for the ways He has worked in you through your relationships. Ask Him to help those around you see Him through your love for them.

A New Name

WHAT CAN I give him more than that? I would give him anything.

"Amanda," Michael said, holding her tenderly. "Tirzah . . ."

Sarah, came the still, soft voice, and she knew the one gift she had to offer. Herself. Angel drew back from Michael and looked up at him. "Sarah, Michael. My name is Sarah. I don't know the rest of it. Only that much. Sarah."

Michael blinked. His whole body flooded with joy. The name fit her so well. A wanderer in foreign lands, a barren woman filled with doubt. Yet Sarah of old had become a symbol of trust in God and ultimately the mother of a nation. Sarah. A benediction. Sarah. A barren woman who conceived a son. His beautiful, cherished wife who would someday give him a child.

It's a promise, Lord, isn't it? Michael felt the warmth and assurance of it enter every cell of his body.

❧

Names have meaning.

The first time Angel met Michael, he asked her what her name was, and she told him to call her whatever he wanted. No one knew her real name—not even Duke—and she didn't plan to change that. It was the only thing she had left of herself, and she guarded it closely.

So Michael took her at her word and called her Mara. Tirzah. Amanda. Names that reflected who she had been and who he hoped she would become. But all the while he longed to know who she really was.

Angel gave him a gift now: the truth of who she was, holding nothing back. Telling him her true name was evidence she trusted him enough to know he would not use the information against her. She was fully his.

When Michael heard her name, he immediately saw parallels with the biblical Sarah, who spent much of her life traveling through other countries—ever the nomad, never at home. She married a man of great faith but seemed to have plenty of her own doubts. God promised Abraham that he would be the ancestor of nations, but Sarah grew tired of waiting and stage-managed, producing a child through her maid, Hagar, instead. Later, when an angelic visitor told Abraham that this time next year Sarah would have a son, her response could hardly be called one of faith: "She laughed silently to herself and said, 'How could a worn-out woman like me enjoy such pleasure, especially when my master—my husband—is also so old?'" (Genesis 18:12, NLT).

Even though she doubted, God was faithful. And when her son was born, she and Abraham named him Isaac, which means "laughter"—surely a joyous reference to God keeping His promises despite her own disbelief. The author of Hebrews even included Sarah in the hall of faith: "By faith even Sarah herself received ability to conceive, even beyond the proper time of life, since she considered Him faithful who had promised" (11:11). Sarah was a flawed woman—aren't we all?—but she learned to trust in a flawless God. Just as Angel had.

Mara, the first name Michael used for Angel, means "bitter." Sarah means "princess." God brought Angel so far from pain and bitterness that she now knew who she really was: Sarah. Precious. Valuable. Daughter of God. Beloved.

These words apply to you too. This is the reality of those who have trusted in Christ to redeem and restore them. This isn't just a happy ending for two characters in a book; it's a happy ending for all believers.

Once we were *rejected,* feeling alone and unloved.

We were *resigned* to our situation, sure change would never come.

But now we are *rescued.* The door to our dungeon has been thrown open, and we are no longer stuck in captivity.

We are *redeemed*—taken by the hand and led to freedom.

We are *reconciled* to God. Our relationship has been repaired.

And now we are being *restored.* God is changing us little by little, and one day, when we see Him face to face, we will be fully the people we were created to be.

The prophet Isaiah spoke words of hope that the Israelites

could hold on to during the time of their exile. Though things were bleak at that time, this passage illustrates how God would restore them—and it also gives us hope for the future:

> You will be given a new name
>> by the LORD's own mouth.
> The LORD will hold you in his hand for all to see—
>> a splendid crown in the hand of God.
> Never again will you be called "The Forsaken City"
>> or "The Desolate Land."
> Your new name will be "The City of God's Delight"
>> and "The Bride of God,"
> for the LORD delights in you
>> and will claim you as his bride. (Isaiah 62:2–4, NLT)

Isaiah wrote that Zion will be given a new name—and what a symbolic one. No longer forsaken or desolate, it will now be loved, delighted in, and chosen. That drastic turn-around describes us as well. Our past will always be with us, but we are no longer captive to it. We have been restored and made new.

I hope that walking through Angel's story has given you a glimpse of God's grace, His forgiveness, and His power to transform our lives. Nothing is too hard for Him. May you draw near to Him and be changed by His amazing, over-whelming, redeeming love.

> I pray that from his glorious, unlimited resources he will
> empower you with inner strength through his Spirit.
> Then Christ will make his home in your hearts as you

trust in him. Your roots will grow down into God's love and keep you strong. And may you have the power to understand, as all God's people should, how wide, how long, how high, and how deep his love is. May you experience the love of Christ, though it is too great to understand fully. Then you will be made complete with all the fullness of life and power that comes from God.

Now all glory to God, who is able, through his mighty power at work within us, to accomplish infinitely more than we might ask or think. Glory to him in the church and in Christ Jesus through all generations forever and ever! Amen. (Ephesians 3:16–21, NLT)

Memorize Ephesians 3:18–20. Recite it to yourself often, and let its meaning permeate your life.

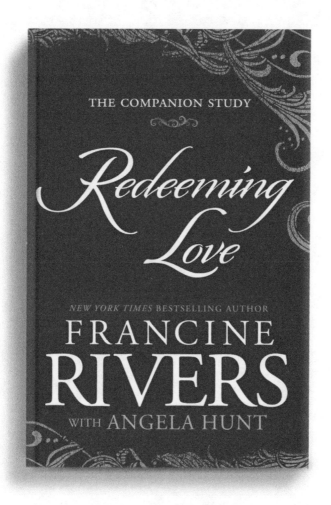

THE COMPANION STUDY

Redeeming Love

NEW YORK TIMES BESTSELLING AUTHOR

FRANCINE RIVERS

WITH ANGELA HUNT

Discover through this six-week Bible study how the
life-changing love celebrated in the Christian classic
Redeeming Love can transform your life.

Follow along on social at @redeeminglovebook

 MULTNOMAH

www.waterbrookmultnomah.com

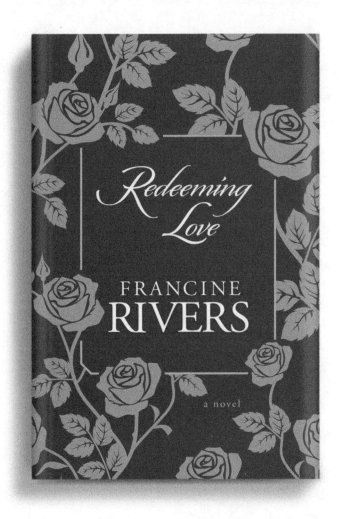

A new collectible edition of the
beloved novel now available

Follow along on social at @redeeminglovebook

 MULTNOMAH

www.waterbrookmultnomah.com